When Your Pet Dies
How to Cope with Your Feelings

"Reading *WHEN YOUR PET DIES* is the next best thing to hearing Quackenbush's wise, gentle, understanding voice. Based on extensive case histories, the book should bring comfort and wisdom to anyone who has recently lost a pet or who is preparing for such a loss."
—*Philadelphia Inquirer*

"Informative . . . will undoubtedly provide comfort for pet lovers who wish to come to terms with their grief."
—*Cats* magazine

"If reading about the emotional odyssey of grieving pet owners—and one man's therapeutic approach to guiding them—gives you a feeling of kinship with other sufferers, then this book is for you. [It] is a small price to pay for such expert counseling."
—*Southern Connecticut Newspapers, Inc.*

"As a pet owner and a professional, I feel this book is an invaluable aid in helping us deal with pet loss."
—*Sally Haddock, D.V.M.,*
author of *The Making of a Woman Vet*

AN ALTERNATE SELECTION OF THE RODALE/PREVENTION BOOK CLUBS

JAMIE QUACKENBUSH, M.S.W., was the nation's first full-time pet bereavement counselor, and was affiliated with the Veterinary Hospital of the University of Pennsylvania. He now lives in Venice, California.

DENISE GRAVELINE is a free-lance writer and former editor of *Pet Care Report*.

When Your Pet Dies

How to Cope with Your Feelings

*Jamie Quackenbush, M.S.W.
and Denise Graveline*

POCKET BOOKS

New York   London   Toronto   Sydney   Tokyo   Singapore

POCKET BOOKS, a division of Simon & Schuster Inc.
1230 Avenue of the Americas, New York, NY 10020

ISBN: 0-671-66930-3

First Pocket Books printing August 1988

10 9 8 7 6 5 4 3

POCKET and colophon are registered trademarks of
Simon & Schuster Inc.

Printed in the U.S.A.

*It is not often that someone comes along
who is a true friend and a good writer.*
—Elwyn Brooks White, Charlotte's Web

*Because Bill Shaw is both, this book is
dedicated to him.*

Acknowledgments

Without the first pet bereavement counseling service, these stories of grieving owners would never have been recorded, studied, or resolved. Particular people and schools at the University of Pennsylvania helped to conceive, develop, and support this valuable service. We especially thank Dean Robert M. Marshak and Dr. Leon Weiss of the School of Veterinary Medicine, and Dean Louise Shoemaker of the School of Social Work, who established the center for the Interaction of Animals and Society, as well as the Geraldine R. Dodge Foundation, which supports the center with funding. Others whom we thank for contributing their expertise to the service include: Professor Eleanor Ryder of the School of Social Work; Dr. Kenneth C. Bovee, former chair of clinical studies, and Dr. Lawrence T. Glickman, chief of epidemiology, both of the School of Veterinary Medicine; and Dr. Victoria L. Voith, director of the school's Animal Behavior Clinic.

We also thank those people who shared their bereavement for pets with us through interviews, letters, and counseling sessions. Many of them hoped that their stories might help other pet owners; their willingness to recall painful events has given this book its shape and substance. Their names, their pets' names, and minor circumstantial details have been changed to protect their privacy; we regret that we cannot thank all of them personally for their vital help.

Our most heartfelt thanks go to Karen Quackenbush and Robert and Monique Graveline, who shared each deadline, rewrite, and concern with patience and support. Our editor, Patricia Soliman, and our agent, Helen Brann, gave us their encouragement and vision. Because they made it both possible and pleasing to write this book, they have not only our thanks but our respect.

J. Q. and D. G.

Contents

Preface

How Pet Bereavement Counseling Works

If you needed my help to cope with the death of your pet I'd start the counseling process with one question: "Why was Baxter so special to you?" I may never have seen your animal, especially if you consult with me by letter or phone call, as many pet owners do. Or I may have just spent an hour or more with you in the emergency-room waiting area while the doctors and technicians at the Veterinary Hospital of the University of Pennsylvania (VHUP) tried to revive your pet after an accident. Perhaps I was standing by you while a veterinarian gave your animal a euthanasia injection to end his life quickly and without pain. Most likely I know only his name and his recent medical history, but it's still obvious to me that he was no ordinary pet—your distress makes that clear. So I ask why.

My simple question usually sparks hours of one-sided conversation because you tell me much more than the animal's breed, age, and history of illness. I want to hear about the habits and happenings of your life with the pet, and I do. I learn that he always slept on your bed or beneath a favorite sunny window; that he begged scraps from everyone at the table or refused anything but a certain food from your hand; that he never barked or always chewed the furniture. I hear about the vacations you took with him and the ones when he stayed behind, the crises he helped you to weather and those he brought about. He amused you, annoyed you, comforted you—he was a member of your family, not just a pet. And as you remember and describe all these day-to-day details, seemingly mundane, you can see for yourself why you're so upset. The loss of such a constant, reliable companion leaves a void that's difficult to fill.

You may not realize it immediately, but you've lost a life-style as well as a friend. Both people and pets are creatures of habit: remember how your dog expected his exercise walk promptly at 6 A.M., rain or shine? Or how your cat always rubbed at your ankles when you came home from work, greeting you at the door? Or some special greeting ritual that evolved between you? Your pet's death brings all this to an abrupt end. The dog no longer requires those walks, the cat isn't there to demonstrate affection as you enter the house, but your need for those comforting, familiar rituals doesn't end immediately after your pet dies. You may not want to get up in the morning without that exercise walk or return to an empty house in the evening. To make matters worse, you're probably feeling confused, embarrassed, or ashamed for letting a pet's death put the rest of your life on hold, even temporarily. And to some extent you may feel angry with yourself—or your pet—because you resent your lack of control over the situation.

If so, you're like the hundreds of bereaved pet owners I counsel every year as the VHUP social worker. Since the first social work and bereavement counseling program began here five years ago, I've found that owners grieve for their pets as intensely as if a human companion had died, with one complicating factor: it's still not widely acceptable to be upset by an animal's death, so you may face not only private sorrow but public bereavement made difficult by others' attitudes. You might suspect that no one understands your feelings when family, friends, or co-workers react to your tears with bewilderment—or even scorn. Perhaps that's why so many pet owners try to struggle through this painful period alone.

You may not, however, feel capable of working through something as disturbing as bereavement all by yourself. In grief it's difficult to step back from the emotional turmoil and calmly look at the social roles, behavior, and environments affecting your feelings. But if someone else can help you gain that perspective you'll be better able to make the decisions to put your life in order. That's what a social worker can do. The need for counseling doesn't imply that bereaved owners are in need of psychiatric help; grief and mourning for either a person or a pet are normal, if harrowing, human experiences. As you come to grips with your feelings and adjust to your pet's death, I'm there to reassure and encourage you. Essentially, I help you to help yourself cope and I do that in three general ways:

Educating You About Death. Much more than the end of a life has occurred. Your pet may have symbolized certain things to you—a companion, a reason for being, comfort, security. Those may seem to disappear when he dies, and a part of you may feel like dying too. The pet helped shape your world, your behavior, your relationships: how are those changed now that he's dead? How do you feel about death—a topic most people try to avoid? Which feelings can you expect? Which are signs of trouble?

Locating Sources of Support. I'm on call at the VHUP twenty-four hours a day precisely so I can be available whenever an owner needs advice or a listening ear. But you'll need to look for supportive people around you as well. You may turn to your spouse or children for comfort. Perhaps a co-worker, friend, or neighbor has gone through a similar experience and is willing to discuss it with you. The key to developing these human resources during this period is to remember that some people will be sympathetic and others will not. Expect some resistance to your feelings, but understand not everyone knew and loved your pet as you did —including members of your own family. They may not share your sorrow, but you can ask them to respect it or, if necessary, simply avoid them for a while.

Learning How to Cope. How do you plan to fill the hours once taken up with your pet's care? How will you gradually alter your daily routines to accommodate life without your pet? How do you handle the decisions regarding his death—choosing a burial method, holding a memorial service? If you have an elderly or terminally ill pet you may have to make some decisions before he dies. Perhaps the most difficult will be euthanasia. And after any pet's death you may wonder about getting another animal. I work with you to ease and clarify those decision-making processes, although you must make the choices. In each case you should pick the option that will make you feel most comfortable in the long run.

Perhaps the most important thing I can do for you during our counseling sessions is to let you know I care. That sounds simple, but most people feel that simple needs are the most vital: to care and be cared for, to sense that others respect their problems and needs. Unfortunately, many bereaved pet owners sometimes encounter only indifference or surprise. When they express their sense of loss they often hear "Why don't you just get another one?" or "It was *only* a pet!" I try a different approach, saying, "I imagine you must really be hurting inside right now." Again, a simple statement, but it starts a bond of enormous trust between us; you know that you can tell me all about your feelings without fear of misunderstanding.

I can be more sensitive to your grief and mourning because I've gone through two similar experiences myself. Oddly enough, both happened during the summer before I began my work and doctoral studies at the University of Pennsylvania. My wife, Karen, and I had been living in a rural area of Michigan with my dogs, Duchess and Taffy, and her cats, Sandra and Funny Face. We returned from a summer vacation to find Funny Face in failing health, steadily losing weight and vitality. Our veterinarian diagnosed the problem as feline leukemia virus, an incurable and debilitating disease that continues to baffle the profession today. In 1979 they knew even less about it; the prohibitive cost and negative prognosis made treating Funny Face untenable.

Karen, who'd owned the cat even before we married, decided it would be best to put him to death. Although she had the courage to choose euthanasia, she couldn't summon enough to take him to the veterinarian for the injection. I wasn't as attached to Funny Face as she, so I volunteered to take him during my lunch hour the next day. I thought this trip would be relatively easy.

On the way to the hospital Funny Face climbed into my lap as we waited at a stop sign. Purring, he put his paws on my chest and looked into my eyes. I started to cry. He'd always been a fat, cuddly cat whom I liked to tease; now he looked completely helpless. Overcome with the thought that I was driving him to his death, I managed to deliver him to our veterinarian, although I couldn't stay with him when he died.

One of my co-workers saw that I was upset and

shared some of his experiences with euthanasia and his dogs. Karen and I had a good cry together when I went home that night. Much later I realized why I'd felt so sad and why it helped to share those feelings: even the teasing and little games I'd played with Funny Face had become rituals I enjoyed and would miss. I found myself deeply regretting the death and the pain it brought our family, even though we had no other choice.

Those feelings helped prepare me for an even harder decision some weeks later. We were nearly ready to move to Philadelphia, but couldn't find a new home with enough room for Duchess, my black Labrador, and Taffy, my golden retriever. They'd need extra walks and playtime to match the exercise they'd had in the country all these years. I wrestled with the choices: find them a new home in Michigan or keep them with us, knowing the demands of school and work would limit my spare time to care for them. It was troubling enough to decide that their Michigan life-style suited them best, but when I started to search for new owners it seemed everyone in our area had too many pets already and no one wanted the added responsibility of two frisky dogs. The week before our move I chose my last resort—entrusting them to the care of our local animal shelter. We'd boarded Duchess and Taffy there during long vacations. But this time we were about to leave for good. The shelter couldn't keep the dogs indefinitely, but the staff promised to delay euthanasia as long as they could to give my dogs a better chance of finding a home.

Weeks later, after our move, my new work with pet owners made more sense because of those two saddening decisions. I could clearly see the different levels of attachment that brought people and pets into caring relationships, and I had a stronger respect for the benefits pets offer their owners. But in those first few months I wasn't working with pet owners at all. The social work program had begun as a joint effort between the university's schools of social work and veterinary medicine to find out whether a social worker could be as useful in an animal hospital as in a human hospital. Many felt the owners most in need would be those with misbehaving animals who brought pets to our Animal Behavior Clinic for corrective treatment.

When it became clear those owners had no need for regular counseling, we began asking the veterinarians on the VHUP staff for their advice. Which owners seemed to have the most difficulty while their pets were in the hospital? The response was nearly unanimous: owners whose pets died—particularly those who'd chosen euthanasia—went through strong and draining emotional processes. And no one was sure what to do to assist or comfort them.

The small-animal hospital at Penn's School of Veterinary Medicine is the nation's third largest; nearly 21,000 small animals are treated there each year, at every hour of the day or night. So in March 1980 I took a full-time position that put me on call twenty-four hours a day at the VHUP. In the first year I helped 130 owners cope with the deaths of their pets. Now about 400 owners a year make use of my counseling. With the help of a social work graduate student, the service averages visits with more than one owner each day. Many more write or call, seeking help from their homes all over the United States and Canada. In the five years since our program began, two more have been established: one at New York City's Animal Medical Center and another in St. Paul at the University of Minnesota's College of Veterinary Medicine.

Now that professionals have been able to observe firsthand the depth and range of pet owners' grief and mourning, and know it is comparable to the process following human deaths, it seems as if this should have been obvious all along. Many people accuse veterinarians, as a group, of insensitivity to their bereaved clients' needs. But these people forget that veterinarians are trained in the science and technology of animal medicine—not in human behavior, psychology, or crisis management. Pet owners too often mask their feelings even from their veterinarians, afraid or embarrassed to burden anyone with their troubles. Now veterinary technicians, students, and practitioners are learning to pay close attention to the people *behind* the pets they treat. It's an important adjustment for these professionals to see a pet's death as an event that alters human lives rather than as a failure of their work.

An important offshoot of my efforts at Penn is teaching both veterinary and social work students about the human and humane aspects of their work, helping them to understand the ethical issues involved in science and medicine, particularly in euthanasia cases, and demonstrating the value of cooperation between the two professions. In return the veterinarians at VHUP and many other animal hospitals now look for potential human difficulties when troublesome cases arrive. Many no longer hesitate to let an owner know they care, to comfort someone in grief, or to recognize when an owner needs more help than they can provide. With their cooperation I can often become acquainted with the owner before the death occurs, and so better help that person prepare for the decisions and feelings to come. I also work with the VHUP staff to make sure each owner clearly understands the diagnoses and treatment his animal has received.

Although the VHUP social work program has helped many owners understand and cope with their grief, thousands are still struggling with bereavement; many will experience it sometime in the future, and are perhaps anticipating it even now. Yet few resources are available to encourage these people to talk about and resolve their feelings when their pets die. It's our hope that this book will establish pet owner bereavement as a human experience that is prevalent, real, difficult, and emotionally upsetting, so that owners won't need to feel embarrassed as well as sad when their pets die. Perhaps, then, the people around them will show more respect and compassion for their grief and mourning.

Jamie Quackenbush
Philadelphia, Pennsylvania

Denise Graveline
New Britain, Connecticut

1

Your Confusing Reactions to Your Pet's Death

". . . one day I came home and Sparky didn't come out to greet me. I found her with her chain wrapped around one of the phone poles lying on the ground —the poles sectioned off her yard area. I guess she got caught somehow, and in trying to dig under the pole to free herself, she must have tightened the chain and choked. I wonder if she suffered and wondered where I was? I know in her last moments she must have been so afraid and so alone, and I couldn't help her."

I can rarely anticipate what will happen next in my work. Most of my cases defy scheduling: a call comes in the middle of the night from a VHUP veterinarian or early in the morning from a lonely owner who used to walk his dog at that hour. Entire families might arrive at my office door at 5:00 P.M. or I might see a crisis brewing as I walk through the emergency service. Whatever the circumstance, I'm swiftly drawn into a bereavement experience, listening as an owner struggles to tell me his feelings. But lately a handful of cases have begun to show up at the same time every day. They arrive with my daily mail, bringing distant owners' heartaches and pain in lengthy letters. Despite their grief these people manage to give me detailed accounts of the events leading to the death, their resulting emotions, and every quality they cherished in the now-dead pet. The painstaking descriptions provide me with an amazing record of the bereavement process. Although I think I'm most helpful when I can actually talk and listen to owners, either in person or on the phone, I believe these letters are equally important to their recoveries. Whether they spend hours wrangling with precise wording or simply free-associate their emotions, the process helps them clarify their feelings. By the time they mail off the letters they have as many clues as I will about what has happened to them.

Janet's letter was one I'll never forget. Buried in the many pages of yellow, lined paper were mentions—just mentions—of two traumatic events she'd weathered in the past year: her father's death and her divorce. Both came as surprises. But this thirty-year-old woman didn't send her letter all the way from Arizona to tell me about those things. Janet's six-year-old cocker terrier, Sparky, had helped her cope with both death and divorce. Now, because of an accident, Sparky was dead.

"I had a dog once before," Janet wrote. "I let her run free and saw her get hit by a car, so I vowed that wouldn't happen to Sparky. Because I don't have a fence, I kept her on a chain near the house. And every day when I arrived home, she'd come out, stretch, and wag her tail.

"Then one day I came home and she didn't come out to greet me. I found her with her chain wrapped around one of the phone poles lying on the ground—the poles sectioned off her yard area. I guess she got caught somehow, and in trying to dig under the pole to free herself, she must have tightened the chain and choked. I wonder if she suffered and wondered where I was? I know in her last moments she must have been so afraid and so alone, and I couldn't help her. I learned a lot about strength when my father died and during my divorce, but I just don't have any strength now. I feel so empty and I don't care much about anything.

"Was she taken from me because I was too dependent on her? What's wrong with that if we were both happy? So many people ask me whether I'll get another dog, but the risk of attachment is too great. Besides, I don't want another dog. I just want Sparky back."

It was easy to see why Janet couldn't consider another dog at that time. Sparky's devoted attention, especially during that last traumatic year, was something she'd never forget and couldn't replace. "Sparky had been mine since she was six weeks old," Janet wrote. "After my unexpected divorce, it was just the two of us. She got me through it. Sparky was always my dog; many times I was accused of loving her more. And I did, because she was always there for me, and she needed me. We shared an unconditional love. When it became just the two of us, somehow she knew I needed her more, so we became more inseparable than ever. She kept me from coming home to an empty house—how *happy* we were to see each other every night!"

Janet had waited three weeks to write me, and although she'd made some decisions on her own, she hadn't yet recovered from the shock of Sparky's death. She was moving from her house to an apartment because "it's just too painful for me to stay here. But packing seems so final—it's almost as if she really didn't die, and might come home again any minute. And if she did, I'd be gone. She's buried not far from here, and I feel like I'm leaving her—walking away. It hurts even to think of her, so I try not to. But I still feel like I'm falling apart. Please help me if you can," she concluded. "I just don't know how to ease the pain."

Janet's primary worries were time and trouble. Why was it taking so long for her to recover from the shock? Did that intense grief mean something was wrong with her? Most pet owners want similar reassurances and solutions to their problems right away. Although I can let them know their feelings are normal and natural, I can't provide a speedy end to the pain. Janet is typical because she didn't understand that her distress was a normal part of the recovery process. Her feelings almost had to be this way, at least for a while, in order for bereavement to take its natural course. The process demands time; you must first see the death as a *real* event, then rearrange your life around the great emotional and social vacuum it creates. No one can tell you exactly how long that can take. The duration of your bereavement depends on many factors: your relationship with your pet, your relationships with family and friends, the circumstances of the death, your attitudes to death, your previous experiences with death, and sometimes additional factors. What's more, this particular experience may differ greatly from previous ones for the very same reasons—different relationships, situations, and perceptions.

As you go through bereavement for a pet, you may feel both helpless and hopeless, as if you can't break out of your grief and don't care to do so. But you *can* help yourself, even during your deepest sorrow, and find hope for your recovery simply by thinking about the death and your reactions to it. If you can see your pet's death as part of a larger picture, understand how universal your feelings are, and realize why you feel as you do, you'll be better able to put your life back together as your mourning subsides.

"Does Anyone Else Feel This Way?"

I've heard it time and time again from bereaved owners: "Nobody understands me. Nobody cares that this happened. Does anyone else feel this way?" Pet owners, for some reason, think of themselves as a minority, when precisely the opposite is true. Of the 80 million or more households in the United States, nearly 60 percent have at least one cat or dog as a part of the family. That's more than 100 million cats and dogs with owners, and only an estimate at that. Strays taken into your home are left out of that statistic. An even more accurate view results when you consider the estimated 45 million pet birds and 125 million pet rabbits, reptiles, and rodents that occupy space in our homes.

Of course some people don't become as attached to their pets as others, and those are less likely to experience a long or intense reaction when their animals die. But because so many people do become deeply fond of their pets, researchers have begun to explore their attitudes. Several different surveys conducted in recent years demonstrate that many owners consider their pets family members and treat them that way—with special foods, toys, homes, attention, rituals, and even clothing. What's more, they seem to trust their pets. Adults as well as children talk to and confide in their dogs and cats, who always seem willing to listen; the owners come to depend on the animals for comfort, company, security, and other benefits. Sadly, one of the better measures we have for the depth of these relationships is bereavement. An owner's heartache for a deceased pet may provide us a clear picture of just how intensely he cared for that animal. An even more poignant testimony comes from people who refuse to acquire another animal after a particular pet's death. No one knows how many people choose to stop being pet owners for this reason, but my work has revealed that many prefer to avoid another intense attachment, accompanied as it is by the pain of one more potential loss.

It's even impossible to pinpoint what kind of person typically cares more about his pets, simply because pet owners are one of the most diverse groups in the United States. Unemployed people and millionaires, men and women, educated people and those who cannot read, spouses and singles, children and elderly people—and all variations in between—own pets. Each creates a personal, unique relationship with the animal; no two owners think of their pets in exactly the same way. When several people share ownership, as you'll see in a later chapter, they still build individual relationships with the pet. To one the dog is a bully, to another a lazy good-for-nothing, and a best friend to a third. Or you may find that one person loves his cat as a constant companion and someone else in the household is violently allergic to cats; sometimes the devoted owner is allergic. I've seen as many variations as there are with human-human relationships.

The range includes people who dote on their large African parrots or tiny parakeets, rabbit owners or reptile owners, gerbil lovers and horse fanciers. The majority of American pet owners keep dogs and cats in their homes; in my work I counsel them most frequently. But I know that, when it comes to human-pet relationships, statistics and stereotypes don't really matter. Your *feelings* count most in my work and in your ownership, whether you keep snakes or Siamese cats. With the exception of people who just don't like animals, or feel only ambivalence toward them, most people who own pets do grieve in some measure when their pets die. It's important to remember that your grief for an animal is a *human* reaction. So many people think bereavement is a weakness or feel they should be ashamed of their sorrow. "I'm too old for this," they say, or "too young," "too mature," and even "too masculine." I try to help them see that grief affects *any* person who cared for a now-dead animal, regardless of gender, age, socioeconomic status, ethnic background, or previous experience.

Society has taught many men to mask emotion, but that doesn't prevent them from mourning their pets' deaths. It does mean, though, that they usually add shame and embarrassment to their trauma. Sometimes, haunted by what they see as unacceptable behavior, bereaved men have a more difficult time with their grief than they normally would; their shame may even eclipse the genuine sorrow they feel. Who says a man can't or shouldn't enjoy a close relationship with his dog or cat? I've seen many adult men cry for their dead or dying pets, and not one seemed weak or ridiculous. Like any other owners, they deserve the opportunity to grieve and mourn the deaths of their special friends.

That same thinking, now antiquated, that allows women to express their reactions to death more freely can create problems as well. Many of the adult women I've counseled sense the condescension beneath the words "Women are *always* emotional about these things." If they, too, are led to believe that openly mourning a pet's death signals weakness, they may feel unnecessarily worse about themselves and the experience. Katharine, one of my correspondents, felt that her grieving for Taddles, a twelve-year-old Manx cat, proved she was going crazy! Halfway through her letter she paused in her description of his fatal disease to write, "I don't want to tell you, but I suppose you should know that I'm forty, unmarried, no children—the typical neurotic female, I guess. I'm embarrassed to tell my family or friends. I know they think I'm crazy, and maybe I am." Later in her letter she mentioned she might not mail it "if I read this over and see just how crazy I am. I read in the article I saw that grief like this is normal, but maybe I am a 'fanatic or obsessive personality,' as it says."

I'm glad Katharine did summon up the courage to mail her letter. It began a marvelous correspondence between us in which I was able to help her see that nothing could be more normal—or *less* fanatic—than grief for her sole companion of twelve years. She needed only to know that someone understood her feelings and that others had experienced the same sorrow. Her relief at realizing she wasn't neurotic or crazy was almost tangible. In my mind, overanalyzing your bereavement responses may be one of the most dangerous, damaging things you can do. It does help to consider and to resolve your feelings, but not to use them as evidence against your sanity, your worth, or your role in the world. *Experience your emotions*, don't fight them or judge them, and ignore people who try to do that for you. No matter who you are, your bereavement over a pet's death is necessary, a natural process that will help you in the long run.

"I Thought He'd Be Around Forever"

Remember when you were five years old and twenty years seemed like forever? Your parents may have seemed ancient, even if they were only in their twenties or thirties. The thought of living that long was almost incomprehensible. When you grew up your perspective shifted and you learned the average human lives to be more than seventy years of age, but you could always point to people who'd lived well past that point. Certainly, you hope to live for many decades. It would be difficult to continue living if you didn't think that way; few care to consider death as an immediate threat to their existence. We all say that life's only certainties are death and taxes, but that doesn't stop anybody from putting off either one.

It's natural to avoid thinking of death and to view it as unpleasant, but those attitudes make you less ready to handle death when it does occur. That's why the term "sudden death" seems almost redundant. Every death seems sudden to those who witness it. Many people say "What a shame" or "How unfair, how awful" when they hear of someone's death—usually because *they* weren't prepared for it.

You may anticipate death with contentment, looking forward to an afterlife of some sort; you can decide whether it will be good or bad. That belief doesn't delay death so much as it softens the blow—a mere transition from one life to the next doesn't seem as final or traumatic. Belief in an afterlife gives you other benefits, too, chief among them the prospect of reunion with family members and friends who've died before you. Any loss through death turns into a temporary parting; your own death looks better because it will bring about a happy reconciliation with loved ones. As unrealistic as those beliefs may seem to agnostics and atheists, they do help others to cope with an otherwise incomprehensible event, and to that extent they're useful—if they're not taken to extremes.

But even if you can accept the inevitability of human

death, you're still likely to falter when your pet dies. I'm not referring to accidental death—the one kind of death that always shocks and surprises you. It's far more common for you to completely misunderstand your animal's life span—so much so that your pet's death, regardless of the cause, catches you unprepared. Few veterinarians would venture to guess how long your pet will live, and for good reason: they realize how short most dog and cat life spans actually are, and they know further that most of you wouldn't believe their estimates. Pet owners usually imagine *their* animals will live for a long, long time, despite what they hear from reliable sources.

Why do people know—or recognize—so little about pets' life spans? Part of the problem lies in the research; we have no actuarial tables from insurance companies to estimate pets' lives, as we do our own. What's more, the characteristics of every breed have evolved dramatically over the centuries, changing expected life spans at the same time; accidents, epidemics, and shifts in animal life-styles also make it difficult for scientists to monitor any pet's complete life. Take poodles, for example. These prized show dogs were once expert retrievers, plunging after downed ducks or geese into lakes and streams for their hunting masters. Now they lead far less strenuous lives, retrieving nothing more than the evening paper, if that. Life-style changes over many years have resulted in risks, diseases, and physical conditions for today's poodle that bear no resemblance to those of his ancestors. For many breeds of cats and dogs, similar life-style shifts may happen so quickly no researcher can keep up with them. The expected life span of a show dog versus a hunter may be very different. But, generally, too many variables exist to allow professionals to gauge those life spans precisely.

Another problem arises from the inaccurate images most owners carry of their pets. Many shocked owners tell me they thought "he'd be around forever" when they first react to a pet's death. From ancient civilization to the present day, a long life has always been something to revere and work toward. The earliest peoples believed certain foods and substances would prolong life; Madison Avenue and the media communicate the same message to both people and pets. It's become an almost romantic thought that you can count on your pet's presence for many, many years—and certainly no one who cares about a cat or dog would want to do anything to shorten his life. So humans sell and buy products linked to prolonging their pets' lives when no such effect can be definitely confirmed. It's a false comfort to think that a particular food, shelter, or product will keep your pet alive longer, no matter how much preparation and information stands behind it. What's more, that kind of misleading advertising works against you if you want to be realistically prepared for your pet's death when it does occur.

You may also rely on folk wisdom about your dog or cat's life span. You can *roughly* estimate how long your pet might live, but first you must forget the old adage that one of his years equals seven of your own—or four, or five, or thirteen, or any other figure you may have heard. A year-old cat or dog is already sexually mature and fully grown, or nearly so; he resembles a young adult more than a five-year-old human. That doesn't give you an accurate yardstick, either, since the first year of a pet's life is one of unusually fast growth and development. Rather than compare your dog or cat's life span to yours, look at his size. In general— *and only in general*—that suggests his average life expectancy. That's perhaps not much comfort to cat owners, I know, since so many feline breeds are of similar sizes. This measuring system has nothing to do with over- or underweight animals but with their average sizes. Dog owners should know that the so-called giant breeds, such as Great Danes and Newfoundlands, have the shortest life spans; some live as few as four years. Large breeds, including Labrador retrievers, Irish setters, and the like, generally live somewhat longer. It's the toy breeds, smallest of all, that tend to live longest. A tiny Chihuahua or miniature schnauzer might live as long as twelve years or even longer. Cat and dog owners may not realize their mixed-breed animals may stand a better chance of longevity than do many purebreds. Other types of pet animals live for shorter or longer spans, calculated in different ways. For birds the size indications show the opposite life-span ranges: a small budgie or parakeet might live for just a few years, while a large, exotic parrot can easily live as long or longer than a human. Of course any pet's life span can be shortened or somewhat prolonged by his health care, exercise, diet, and contact with communicable diseases, as well as his general physical safety. Size is only a general indicator of the years an animal has to live, but by no means solely determines them.

It's far easier for you to believe folk tales about animal life spans than the medically based guidelines I've just given you. If you think your cat's year equals five human years and he dies at fifteen, you can comfort yourself that he lived to be seventy-five in human terms —what we consider to be a "ripe old age." Even if you don't cherish those well-worn estimates, I'm well aware that every pet you've owned or known may have lived past the estimated ages I mentioned, size or no size. What about your fifteen-year-old Lab, your twenty-year-old Siamese? I can't tell you why they exceeded normal medical expectations, but you're fortunate they did. At first it may seem awful that a Great Dane may live only four to six years; to you, that's a relatively short time. However, once you remember that a Great Dane doesn't have an education, a career, a family, or hobbies to pursue, four years may seem more adequate for his life. He's on a very different time schedule than you are, as are all your pets. Think of it this way: wouldn't you rather be pleasantly surprised that he did live so long than be sadly shocked at his short life? The only upsetting thing about your pet's relatively brief life span is that you're ill prepared to accept it. You can save yourself many hours of regret later if you begin to look realistically at his longevity now.

Four Common Reactions to a Beloved Pet's Death

I've told you the bereavement process takes time and that the time will vary from person to person. But you may feel so many conflicting responses to your pet's death that it seems they'll take forever to resolve. You can expect always to feel some sorrow and regret for your loss, no matter how many years go by; the challenge you face is to deal with the different kinds of emotional pain you feel, to make them manageable rather than attempt to avoid or ignore them.

Your distressing reactions to death have been described in the landmark work *On Death and Dying* by Elisabeth Kübler-Ross, who has studied human responses to human death for a number of years. She observed five different responses that both the dying and the bereft may experience: *denial, anger, bargaining, depression,* and *acceptance.* With just a slight variation, such responses are identical in humans' bereavement for their pets. I have rarely seen the *bargaining* phase; however, I almost always see owners go through an additional reaction, guilt. So in many ways you can expect to grieve for your pet much as you would for a human family member.

But just as Janet's feelings came tumbling out in no particular order as she wrote her letter, your feelings won't necessarily follow a predictable pattern. You might be angry about your pet's death for five minutes, then feel both guilty and depressed for two weeks—yet never try to deny or delay acknowledgment of the death. Or you may feel only a crushing depression. Denial might wipe out any other reaction. You can alternate those emotions, bouncing from one to the next, or experience them all at once. That's why the healing process is so confusing. You might be able to identify each feeling, as Janet did, but find that none of them is confined to a specific, orderly time period. Many professionals speak of bereavement stages, but I'm not completely comfortable with that notion; even a professional can't predict how long each stage will endure, its level of intensity, or when it will occur, if ever. You can define bereavement only in terms of where and how *your* feelings find expression: privately, in grief, and publicly, in mourning.

Janet felt as if she was falling apart for several reasons. Most probably her life had been a predictable mix of ups and downs, none too severe. Then she lost her father, her husband, and her dog in quick succession. Each of her reactions came as swiftly and surprisingly as Sparky's accidental death. That's a frightening situation for an adult who usually expects to act and react in a mature and rational manner. Like Janet and Katharine, you may mistrust and fear the most natural reactions to death because those powerful emotions are unlike anything you've ever experienced before.

Feeling Guilty: "And I Couldn't Help Her"

Guilt may be the most common feeling that torments you, and the reasons are usually simple: you feel responsible for your pets' well-being. He's entirely dependent on you for food, shelter, health care, exercise, attention, and affection. He can't voice his needs as a human does or fend for himself as a wild animal does. When he's young you worry because he's not yet familiar with the dangers of the world around him; as he ages he may forget or fail to comprehend those risks. So when he dies it may seem as if you could or should have done something more to help him. Or you may feel you could somehow have prevented his death, however unrealistic that might be.

Those are caring and noble sentiments—and they put you in an uncomfortable position. If you've always told your pet "I'd do anything to keep you from harm" you may remember those words when he dies and feel full of failure and regret. It must have been your fault, some oversight on your part, your selfishness that contributed to his demise. Your nagging conscience tells you you're guilty, giving you the clearest hindsight with which to view your mistakes. In the end, when he needed you most, you didn't live up to your responsibility to care for your dog or cat. You may think that can mean only one thing: you've been a bad owner to a pet you dearly loved.

Now, few people come to guilt after such a straightforward line of reasoning. You may not actually think it through that way, but it's basically the way you feel. Regardless of what causes your guilt, that haunted reaction most likely echoes Janet's thoughts: "I know in her last moments she was so afraid and so alone, and *I couldn't help her*."

Marty, a thirty-two-year-old Canadian, wrote about his husky, Katch, in almost the same words, but from a different point of view. Katch had a debilitating terminal disease rather than an accident. "The nerve cells in his back gave out," Marty wrote. "He simply couldn't lift his hind quarters off the floor. . . . He knew something was wrong, and, as he had all his life, he turned to me for help. But *there was nothing I could do*, and that devastated me."

Both Marty and Janet were berating themselves for their respective failures when they wrote me, but they also unwittingly described what will someday free them from their guilt. There honestly *was* nothing either of them could do—no way they could have known, no reason they would have done things differently, no moment they can now change. A more appropriate, positive way of expressing that is "I did everything I could." But when something as helpless as a sick or injured animal dies, and you can't stop the death, it's natural to think only in negatives as the bereavement process begins.

That's why I try to help pet owners who feel this guilt acknowledge that they have done everything within reason. It's usually the truth, too, and not just a consoling thing to say. Jack, a devoted cat owner, is a New Jersey resident in his early forties. After his twelve-year-old cat died he told me, "I always thought of Felix first— what were his needs? He was more helpless than I; his meals had to come before my happy hour drink or my movie. Then, and only then, I'd decide what to do for myself. He needed me." Numerous pet owners have told me they'd "do anything" for their animals, and they try to reach that goal every day. They rise early in the morning to walk the dog, buy all manner of toys to amuse the cat, construct elaborate homes for gerbils and birds, make sure their animal gets special medical care and food, and move heaven and earth to find him when he's lost. I'll bet you're not much different. Those daily chores are active demonstrations of your love for your pet; when those caring acts can no longer keep him alive, you'll certainly feel both helpless and regretful, if not to blame.

But you must make an important distinction here. You may *want* to do anything for your pet but you're *able* only to do everything you can—and no more. Janet's devotion and care for Sparky were complete, but she still feels she failed to meet her dog's needs. That guilty feeling carries over from her first dog's death as well, even though she acted in her pets' best interests both times. She let her first dog run free, probably thinking he would enjoy running without restraint—until the dog ran right into the path of an oncoming car. Janet learned from that experience and made the sensible decision to put Sparky on a chain, but even that killed her dog. Are these deaths really Janet's fault? I have a great deal of difficulty placing blame on any owner who performs a caring act based on good intentions, even one that ends in an unfortunate result. Janet cared for her dogs far too much to ever knowingly jeopardize their health or welfare, much less their lives. She now must struggle to make sense of senseless tragedy: how could such an awful thing happen to her Sparky? Because no clear facts or reasons exist, she blames herself, the one person obviously responsible. This is a normal and expected part of the healing process. That may be easier to understand when you consider how intently Janet focused on Sparky's care. The dog needed her love, and she cherished the opportunity to give it. But Janet and many other pet owners need to realize that death isn't always reasonable—it is, in fact, often random and apparently senseless. No owner can spend every waking moment ensuring his animal a safe and happy life, any more than he can do so for himself. Even if you could give up your job, relationships, obligations, meals, and sleep, your pet still might have a fatal accident or terminal disease. If you've been doing everything you can to keep him well and safe, you realize just by doing these things that your capabilities are limited. Your pet's death is most likely not your fault at all (even though it may feel that way), but his death *is* your loss. *Of all times, you need to be kind to yourself during bereavement* for your dog or cat, focusing on all that you *were* able to do for him. I would be surprised if your continued good efforts weren't considerable contributions to his happiness and well-being.

Feeling Angry: "How Could You Do This to Me?"

The feeling that someone or something is to blame for your pet's death is natural, even if you don't accuse yourself of it. With the great advances made in medicine, engineering, law, and the sciences, it seems we should have an answer to everything. But the reason for death is so simple it's difficult to accept: *every living thing must die.* With rare exceptions, the manner and cause of each death remain unknown until it occurs. Even with that in mind, you may ask "Why did it have to happen?" and no one has a satisfactory answer—that is, one to make you feel immediately better about the

death. That's frustrating, a feeling that often comes out
as *anger* in bereaved owners. If you can accuse someone of your pet's death, or hold someone responsible,
you'll feel good and bad at the same time. Your anger or
frustration won't change the facts or the pain, but you'll
feel relieved that you can determine and understand the
cause of death. You have a target on which to ventilate
your pain and rage.

It's normal for you to feel this way, considering how
you cared for the cat or dog you loved so well. You
couldn't control what happened to him, and you may
feel your caring and companionship were stymied for
very unfair reasons. Perhaps you had to be away from
him when he died—at work, on vacation, or simply
doing an errand. Or you may be overwhelmed by the
medical complications of a terminally ill pet, frustrated
by the hospital's inability to tell you more about his disease. So you could easily be angry with your boss, your
family, your responsibilities, or your veterinarian for
keeping you away from him when it would seem, as
Janet said, he was "so alone." It doesn't matter at whom
you hurl that anger, or how long the feeling lasts; this
reaction may surprise you more than any other and
prompt you to do unexpected and uncharacteristic
things. I've seen pet owners kick cars, punch walls,
write venomous letters, hang up the phone on their best
friends, and push for legislation to reform animal hospitals, all in their frustration over a pet's death and circumstances they were unable to control.

That angry reaction stems as much from your shock
as anything else. If the death takes you by surprise, your
perception of it as unfair and wrong may be heightened.
When Louise, a woman in her early fifties, brought her
Cairn terrier, Mitzi, into the VHUP one day, she was
simply following her veterinarian's suggestion to have

the dog tested for thyroid problems. What would have been a routine examination became complicated when the series of tests prompted Mitzi's placement in the intensive care unit. She was in such poor condition, with multiple problems the severity of which our clinicians could only estimate, that they felt she required medical care before she could ever withstand the tests.

I sat with Louise in the reception area, talking about the situation and learning how she felt about the issues she might face. She was terrified she might have to choose euthanasia for Mitzi; she just wasn't ready for that decision. The terrier had been hers for thirteen years—her longest and most reliable relationship ever. As she put it, "Even my marriage, which is breaking up right now, didn't last that long." Just then one of the veterinarians in charge of Mitzi's care came in to tell us that the dog had died of cardiac arrest. Louise's immediate and overwhelming reaction was one of relief. She'd been spared a decision she feared, and Mitzi was finally "at peace," as she told me. She went to see her dog before leaving the hospital and kept saying how fortunate it was that Mitzi would be spared the ordeal of arduous tests and uncomfortable treatments.

Within twenty-four hours, however, her mood changed to anger and frustration. Her soon-to-be-divorced husband accused her of neglect of the dog; her supervisor at work brushed off her concern about arranging for Mitzi's burial and ignored Louise's request to take an afternoon off for it. With little support to help justify her feelings, she forgot how welcome Mitzi's manner of death had seemed. Instead, she lashed out at her husband, fumed silently at her supervisor, and began to review in her mind all the medical concerns the VHUP doctors had expressed about Mitzi. Why hadn't her *own* veterinarian noticed those conditions? The

VHUP staff had seen immediately that the dog was critical; if her veterinarian had been alert, she might yet have Mitzi with her to provide the comfort so lacking from her husband and her supervisor. In that roundabout manner Louise focused the blame—and all her frustration—quite mistakenly on her veterinarian.

I continued to call Louise at her home in Maryland as she began to work through the decisions for Mitzi's burial. As she started the bereavement process, her anger at her veterinarian simply vanished. She found that her father and one of her neighbors were understanding and supportive; her own physician was made aware of her heightened depression and sadness and was able to help her too. With those sources of caring and concern, Louise found she could focus on what was troubling her most—the loss of her special friend and faithful dog.

Veterinarians aren't the only people you may want to blame for your pet's death, although they are, unfortunately, almost always considered somewhat responsible. Your pet's doctor probably will be the first to admit he doesn't—and can't—know everything about animal medicine, yet you may still expect unlimited knowledge and expertise. You may consider veterinarians in the role of healer, with a charge to make sick and injured animals well. Often they can do no more than amend problems temporarily, give relief from pain, prolong an organ's ability to function, and monitor any further complications. They can't prevent death in many cases, and may not be able to anticipate it any better than you. This happens because there are limits to what veterinary medicine can accomplish, even for a pet you consider special. Remember, too, that your veterinarian may be a general practitioner rather than a specialist; he may not have access to the latest information, technology, or equipment. That's exactly why Louise's veterinarian referred her to the VHUP. He knew his limits and wanted Mitzi to receive the most enlightened care. I think most veterinarians feel frustration and loss when they're unable to save your pet's life because they consider their helplessness a failure.

But suppose your veterinarian *has* been helpful, doing all he could until the moment your animal died? Who else might receive the brunt of your anger? Louise was angry at her husband and her boss, not because they had anything to do with the death, but for their insensitivity to it. That added insult to her hurt. You might also find yourself angry with the pet who died, thinking "How could you be so stupid, running right in front of that car after all the time we spent on obedience training?" or "You knew that cabinet was off limits. But you still broke into it and drank the cleaning fluid!" or simply "How can you leave me like this, just when I need you the most?" I know this last reaction can be terribly upsetting. Feeling angry at a helpless companion who had no say in his time or manner of death may only increase your sorrow or guilt.

Particularly where your pet is concerned, your reaction often consists more of frustration than rage. Just as you would with guilt, remember the person or pet that angers you was most likely unaware of and unable to control the situation. The pet may not have known any better, in the case of an accident; if he died of a terminal illness, he had no clear way to communicate his ailment to you. If you can realize your own limits and understand you are not necessarily responsible for his death, you can also apply that thinking to the people around you—your family, friends, or your veterinarian. Death is both awkward and unavoidable for everyone—a frightening and frustrating experience to witness. What may at first seem like neglect, cruelty, or meanness may just be someone's inability to comprehend, cure, or communicate about the end of a pet's life.

Denial: "It's as if She Might Come Back"

Just as anger can be best described as frustration for bereaved owners, the *denial* response really serves as a delaying tactic. You know your pet has died; like most bereft owners, you can't quite believe it. But you take that incredulous feeling one step further—you refuse to believe it or put off thinking about it. You prefer to cling to the hope it might have been a mistake.

This isn't as odd or problematic a feeling as it may seem, unless you take it to extremes. Many people are so stunned by the death and their powerful reactions that they quite naturally wish everything could be as it had been. No matter how mischievous, ill, or troublesome your pet, you'd rather have him alive. It's much easier that way. So you might just temporarily delay any acknowledgment that your animal has died as an easier method of handling all those strong feelings.

For most people, denial or delaying acceptance is an immediate and almost fleeting reaction. You must face the death's reality when you, the hospital, or the pet cemetery disposes of the body, and most people prefer to handle that within twenty-four to forty-eight hours. But even after your pet is buried or cremated, you may find yourself pretending or hoping he's still around—not constantly, but in behavior that approximates forgetfulness. Even Janet, whose letter proved she was clearly aware of Sparky's death, mentioned these small delaying tactics: "The packing seems so final—it's almost as if she didn't really die and might come home any minute. And if she did, I'd be gone." Janet knows Sparky won't be back; her next line told me the dog was "buried not too far from here." But her denial is mild and momentary—"it's *almost* as if"—and very much tied to her feelings of guilt for letting Sparky down in her final hour.

Other small, emotional delaying tactics might include setting out the animal's supper every night, calling out to him, or imagining you hear a scratch at the door or his plaintive call to you. Some of these reactions are not denial but simple habit. Again, they're normal if not taken to extremes. Didn't you do those things for years while your pet was alive? You can't break habits in five minutes; you have to let go of your relationship with your pet gradually. But you should be alert to any sign that this behavior has become unrealistic denial.

It may be more difficult for you to accept your pet's death as a reality if you were somehow prevented from seeing either the actual incident or the body later on—although if you have the choice and prefer not to see either one, that's fine too. If you brought your dog into the VHUP, as Louise did, expecting only routine tests and a quick discharge from the hospital, your pet's death would come as a complete shock. That's exactly why the veterinarians and I let Louise know what was happening as soon as it occurred, and why, as with all pet owners, we offered to let her see Mitzi after the death. If there's a missing link in the information you receive about your pet's treatment and subsequent death, you may well feel he really *isn't* dead.

As with all your reactions, it helps to talk to someone —a veterinarian, counselor, or family or friends, if they're supportive—when you can't bring yourself to admit your pet is gone. That acknowledgment is both simple and horrifying; if you can find someone to reaffirm it for you in a caring way, the process may be gentled. Consider, too, that denial may be no easier than admitting the death occurred, because you're in effect denying yourself the chance to feel bad about this devastating change in your life. The healing process provides you with reason and room to let your feelings out rather than disguise them or hide them away, and I think you'll feel better if you take advantage of an opportunity to release those feelings.

Depression: "I Just Don't Care About Anything Now"

Depression is almost as widespread as guilt among those whose pets have died, but while your conscience pricks at you painfully to remind you of your guilty feelings, you can easily fail to recognize depression. That's because you don't want to notice anything. You're listless, ambivalent, perhaps just melancholy. You don't care; the only reason you bother to eat, sleep, or get up in the morning is that you're supposed to do all those things, not because you take any pleasure in them. If you notice you lack any sort of motivation since your pet died, you're just one of many pet owners who experience depression.

Depression may be the most normal part of the grieving process because it's almost inseparable from loss. You can expect to go through it whenever you lose something that plays a central role in your life— whether it's a spouse, a friend, a job, a livelihood, a skill, or your pet. With that significant part of your life suddenly gone you might well wonder whether you'll ever feel happy again.

That's how your reasoning progresses when you're depressed, but what about your feelings? You don't really go numb, as you might when you're so shocked your feelings seem to freeze in place. Instead, your emotions level off; you pull them into yourself and withdraw from a world that might expect you to share or explain them. You're probably quieter, more pensive, and generally more sad. You may notice that you are lethargic, that you have trouble sleeping or eating on a regular schedule, and you may cry a lot. But you really don't have to look for symptoms—you know better than anyone when you're just down and out, and that's the quality of depression common to bereavement. I don't mean to imply you'll lock yourself in your room, refuse to speak to anyone, or stop bothering to bathe and change your clothes every day. You simply want to disassociate yourself from the rest of the happy, functioning world. You don't *want* to be happy, you don't *want* to function, and there isn't much anyone can say or do to make you feel better about what happened.

The people around you will probably wonder what's wrong with you, particularly if you are usually outgoing and gregarious. But it's normal to withdraw and to feel depressed at this time. You must feel bad in order to feel better, and you may well prefer to do that by yourself. When you're thinking about the pet you've lost, wondering how his death will change your life, privacy can be very important. That's what I told Janet. Look again at her letter, where she writes, "I just don't have any strength now. I feel so empty and I don't care much about anything." Then she shares some of the thoughts that fill her mind when she's alone: "Was she taken from me because I was *too* dependent on her? What's wrong with that if we were both happy? So many people ask whether I'll get another dog, but the risk of attachment is too great. . . . I just want Sparky back."

A Denver man's letter described similar thoughts he had the day after his German shepherd, Jake, died of a heart attack that he "couldn't see coming." Peter wrote,

"I'm feeling pretty cheap and dumb to lose such a friend—all the good times we had don't make it any easier. The house seems so large, echoing, and empty, and the mornings and evenings are especially hard to take. Jake used to get up just to watch me get ready for work in the morning, and I always played with him while I got dressed. He especially liked cookie-keep-away. I just look around and expect him to be there and all I have is cold, empty space." Susie, a twenty-three-year-old Virginia woman, was equally despondent. Her five-month-old pup had died of parvovirus, a swift-moving disease that's often fatal to younger dogs. "I know I only had him for three months, but I'd become very attached to Blade," she wrote. "I still cry when I think about him, which is all the time. I'm single, and I miss his great company."

Life doesn't have much to offer Janet, Peter, or Susie right now, judging by the number of times they refer to the feelings of emptiness and loss that surround them. They don't seem to care about anything except their pain—a painful thought in itself—but that's still the best way they can deal with these regretable deaths.

People who observe this form of depression in you—perhaps members of your family—may fear that the crying, withdrawal, and emptiness may all prompt you to do something drastic, even something as extreme as contemplating suicide. The urge to end your life in response to your pet's death is highly unusual, in my experience. Pathological depression rarely arises in the course of grief for a human or for a pet. Withdrawal and feelings of emptiness are, however, reactions you should expect. Life may not have much to offer you, Janet, Peter, or Susie right now, but that usually means you lack something you cherished—and the sheer loneliness is overwhelming. When I hear a bereaved pet owner say "I feel there's nothing left to live for," he's almost always expressing that loss of special companionship. He rarely means "I want to take my own life," which is a dangerous statement that indicates that the person requires immediate professional attention.

You and your family and friends may wonder just how long you'll be depressed, and that's difficult to gauge. Much depends on the situation, your personal social and emotional context for this death. Janet, for instance, may take a longer time to recover due to the three major losses she experienced over a brief period. She has more than Sparky's death to feel depressed about. The most important thing you can do to effectively handle depression from the loss of a pet is to let it run its course. Ask your family and friends to let you grieve alone for a while, to give you an opportunity to distance yourself, until you're ready to share your feelings. I can't estimate how long it will be until you're able to break out of this circle, since depression affects each person differently. But I can tell you that this pervasive, helpless, and hopeless reaction does serve a positive purpose in your bereavement. It gives you *time* to think about your pet's death and to *put it in realistic perspective*—a perspective you'll require to fully come to grips with the death.

2
Thinking About Your Relationship with Your Pet

"I knew something was wrong as soon as I woke up and couldn't hear Gypsy playing around the room. I rushed her to a veterinarian, even though I knew she was dead beyond any doubt . . . I owe everything to that cat. She's the only reason I've made it this far, the only force that really helped me turn my life around when everything seemed beyond help. I'd be nowhere without her—and that's almost how I feel now that she's dead."

I rarely get to know the animals involved in the person-and-pet relationships I hear about, but I learn intriguing things about those pets' human counterparts. Somewhere in our talks I discover each person's age, marital status, family makeup, and other personal details, but I'm far more interested in the man or woman behind those sketchy facts. My work has taught me to expect the unexpected, to never assume that society's stereotypes and prejudices hold true. That's because my case-history files are full of people with advanced degrees but no common sense; shy, tentative people who assert their consumer rights so the entire hospital can hear them; and staid, correct people who completely lose control of their emotions when they grieve. Bereavement has an amazing impact on people, and no one can predict its intensity. If that were possible I'd be able to work with owners in an unvarying sequence, as if my work were an assembly-line process. But I know I'm usually more effective when working one-on-one. Pet owners' unique and individual qualities inevitably demand that focused attention.

Sometimes my impressions turn to admiration, as they did with Meg. At twenty-eight this elementary schoolteacher had had one of the most troubled lives I've ever encountered. But her story was compelling rather than pitiful; she showed me how much strength people can generate in times of difficulty, and how a special relationship with a pet can help that strength to grow.

When we met, Gypsy, her fluffy gray Persian, had just died of cardiac complications at age nine. Meg's feelings for her cat were unusually intense and devoted. "I owe everything to that cat," she kept saying to me. "She's the only reason I've made it this far, the only force that *really* helped me turn my life around when everything seemed beyond help. I'd be nowhere without her—and that's almost how I feel now that she's dead." Her overpowering gratitude eclipsed every other reaction to her cat's unexpected death, perhaps because its roots lay in events that occurred long before Gypsy ever entered her life. As Meg recalled the experiences she'd endured over the past ten years, with and without the cat, I was amazed, unable to do much more than listen.

Meg had been planning her wedding almost exactly ten years ago, when she was eighteen. Her fiancé had been her high school sweetheart; they graduated, got engaged, and decided on a wedding immediately. Caterer, organist, priest, and photographer had all been contacted; gifts were arriving even as the invitations went out. Then her fiancé's draft notice arrived, just two months before the wedding day. His assignment to Vietnam at the height of the war not only canceled the wedding but put Meg's life on hold, because he was killed in combat soon after his departure.

It didn't seem real to Meg. Her life, and her fiancé's death, sounded like the plot for a harrowing movie. She spent weeks sitting stunned and silent in her parents' home in Maine, seeing only them. But with their support and the encouragement of her high school friends, Meg took tentative steps toward resuming her life, even though it seemed her grief would never subside. She feared loving anyone as much as she had her fiancé; fortunately, her friends didn't try to force her to conform socially. "They didn't care if I was completely quiet and didn't throw myself into what was going on," she recalled. "All they insisted on was my presence at their dinners, or on an occasional weekend trip. At least I got out of the house, moved, saw things happening—it was nice to be included."

Perhaps her most trusted companion and confidant at that time was a man who'd known her and her fiancé in high school. He took Meg out to dinner every week—"really the only kind of 'date' I could handle at that point," she told me. "I'd never felt any pressure from him; he knew all about the horrors, the nightmares. I thought he was my strongest supporter." But then this friend betrayed her trust in the worst possible way: on one of their dates he raped her. And Meg went into another, far more severe emotional tailspin.

Although she confided in her parents, Meg refused to talk about the rape to anyone else. She withdrew into herself, carrying on continual internal conversations. As she meandered aimlessly around the hills surrounding her home, questions came more readily than answers. Could she ever trust another man? Another person? Could any of her hopes come true? Or would she meet with yet another devastating experience? She couldn't risk a relationship, even a friendship, after what had happened. She suspected that another major setback would ruin her emotionally for good. As she mulled over her life Meg came to the conclusion that her ventures into adulthood—from marriage to friendship—were doomed to failure. All of them had ended in pain. At twenty she resolved that she should withdraw from the world to avoid any further risks. She decided to enter a convent, a place where no one could hurt her.

Once again, Meg shared her thoughts with her parents. Their reaction to this latest plan was guarded: did she really believe that escape was a legitimate reason to join a religious order? She did. And then Gypsy showed up.

The newborn kitten came from an oversized litter on a neighboring farm, brought home by Meg's parents specifically to cheer her up. She insisted that her decision was final, but they sensed her despair; perhaps she'd reconsider, they thought, if she had something to care for. Meg didn't have much choice in the matter of becoming Gypsy's friend because the kitten wouldn't leave her alone. Meg's parents were at work all day, and she had no desire to leave the house. So as she watched television, napped, or walked, the kitten followed, curling up by her side or nipping at her shoelaces. Meg began to take responsibility for Gypsy's meals, her litter training, and her amusement. She found herself laughing for the first time in months, for no reason except Gypsy's antics.

Slowly, Meg found she could enjoy life again—perhaps she *had* a future in the world after all. She started thinking about a career, and finally settled on a four-year degree program in education in Boston. When she moved there to start school she took Gypsy along. "I didn't know anyone in the city," she recalled, "and my apartment was as different from home as could be. But Gypsy made me feel better and more confident about those changes; just having her with me helped. She'd sit on my notes, and she loved to march across my typewriter keyboard just when I was typing up term papers. Little things like that kept me going." When Meg completed her degree she took a teaching position at a northern New Jersey school. Gypsy joined in her celebration and made another move with her.

Although the cat was of course older and larger than the kitten she'd first loved, Meg continued to rely on Gypsy's affection. Her companionship comforted Meg after hectic days of teaching first-graders. And as Meg occasionally reassessed her life she always felt grateful for Gypsy's presence. The eight years since they'd become friends were years Meg wouldn't have changed or traded. She never considered their friendship might suddenly stop, as it did when Gypsy died of a heart attack in the middle of the night.

"I knew something was wrong as soon as I woke up and couldn't hear her playing around the room," Meg said. "I rushed her to a veterinarian, even though I knew she was dead beyond any doubt." She took the cat's body back to her parent's property for the burial and stayed on for a few weeks to be with her parents and to think about her loss. The old pain and the old questions came back, but this time Meg couldn't say that her venture into the world had failed. It worked because of Gypsy, she thought. She wasn't out of control in her grief, and she had her parents' understanding and support. But they saw how inconsolable and perplexed she remained about the cat's death and suggested she talk to me.

Meg flew to Philadelphia for a weekend visit and we spent several hours together in my office. What struck me most were her continual references to Gypsy's courage and influence; to me, Meg had shown *just* as much strength in tackling and changing her own life. To help her see the relationship as a joint venture—a shared experience—I asked her to think about and describe the special, small moments when she felt Gypsy had been most helpful. They were the times I've just recounted for you, points at which Meg faced tough choices. By analyzing her relationship with Gypsy carefully, Meg came to see that she, as well as her cat, could take credit for her successes. Understandably, Meg will probably always think of her relationship with Gypsy as a valuable catalyst, an inspiration to live, and an opportunity to regain love and trust. But now she'll do so realistically. If Meg hadn't thought about why and how her cat became so important in her life, she might not have resolved her grief so successfully.

Meg knew she couldn't find that undemanding affection and unswerving devotion in any human friend, particularly after her fiancé's death and her friend's betrayal. But most owners aren't aware their pets offer them an unusual type of friendship that's unavailable elsewhere. It's an easy benefit to miss, since most owners almost assume the friendship is present and then proceed to forget it. Here's how it happens: in any social system of two or more people, your relationship springs from patterns of action and reaction. You know that if you say or do one thing, the other person or persons are likely to respond in a certain way. Those patterns become so predictable after a time that you respond to them unconsciously. In some sense you behave on an automatic level, responding and expecting responses based on that person's role or status in your life.

Your automatic responses can be thrown off course, however, when someone fails to meet your expectations, acts inconsistently, or causes some inevitable conflict. You're shocked at his behavior—you thought he wouldn't act that way based on what you know of him. Relationships with pets lack that element of surprise and conflict. Animals take on unusual roles in our lives, usually those that our perceptions create; your pet can be whatever you want him to be, and generally will never fail to meet your expectations. What's more, you control a pet's actions and reactions to a large extent, since you can train him to respond in a way that best meets your needs. By his nature and the nature of his life-style with you, a pet stays with you in good times and bad, always listens to you, and usually acts as if he understands and sympathizes with what you're saying. Human friends can't be that reliable all the time, but pets can. As a result your pet contributes to your sense of social stability. He's predictable, dependable, giving you a critical sense of emotional balance on an everyday basis.

That's why so many people take pleasure in their pet's companionship. Isn't it comforting to know that at least *one* of your relationships won't involve arguments, disappointments, disagreements, and betrayal? Just by virtue of his inability to speak, your pet eliminates all sorts of potential relationship problems. What's more, you don't have to think too much about that relationship on a day-to-day basis. You need not anticipate difficulty; he's too predictably easygoing for that. So you may almost take your pet's companionship for granted.

The relationship becomes, in fact, so predictable that, like Meg, you may never consider its end. And I don't think you want to anticipate your pet's death constantly because it would sap all the pleasure from the relationship. It's important, however, to think carefully about the nature of your friendship with your animal during your mourning for him. As you recall all the moments you shared you'll understand your reactions to his death and discover the true worth of his contributions to your life. Those insights, however harrowing in the recall, will spur the resolution of your bereavement, but you'll find your relationship with your pet isn't *really* over until you've thought it through, finding and acknowledging clues to his significant role in your life.

The key to my work lies in helping you see the different levels of affection you held for that beloved pet. Only you can provide the details, the highly personal memories, feelings, and benefits you enjoyed. As a careful and supportive observer, I can, however, point out the influences and effects those qualities had on your life, results you may not consciously have been aware of. The combination of those factors gives you an understanding of your companionship that may be your greatest comfort during this time.

What Kind of Companion Was Your Pet?

When you sit down to write a letter do you first review the alphabet, then think of how words are spelled, and finally practice basic grammar? Of course not. You pick up a pen and think of your message, often writing down what first comes to mind. But you don't waste time dissecting or reviewing all the information you know about writing letters; you simply know it and put it to use.

Every day you interact with your pet in much the same way. When you wake up in the morning you don't say to yourself "I have no reason or desire to get up right now, but I'm going to, because the only affectionate relationship I have—the only reason I keep going—is my dog, Jasper. Because he's here, my life has purpose and meaning." You just start your day, probably because Jasper is whining for his breakfast at the foot of your bed. When you walk him you most likely don't consider how calm you'll be as you guide him around the block; you just hook his leash to his collar and go. You feel the benefits instinctively. But to understand that relationship and those benefits you have to go back to the basics of your interactions with a pet. Don't just let the memories go through your mind—put them in perspective. What do you remember best? Why? What did your pet do that made you angry, sad, happy? What did you do to accommodate him in your life? Why did you do those things?

I know you'll be able to think of many such moments because pets take part in almost all their owners' social rituals, from the mundane to the very special. Your pet watched you get dressed every morning before you went to work, but he also saw you prepare for elegant evenings out; he sat under the table during both ordinary meals and festive holiday dinners. He ate his regular meals and stole the cupcakes you made for the school bake sale, wore down the carpet where he napped every day and mischievously gnawed the molding along the wall. You paraded him down the street every night, stopping to show him to passersby, and made every effort to sneak him into your motel room on vacations. You scolded him and held birthday parties in his honor. From all those various rituals and escapades you can draw not only glimpses of the past but a distinct viewpoint on him. Describe him to yourself, or to someone else, and think about what you say: "He was everything to me," or "He was my son's best pal," or "I could always count on him," or "What a troublemaker!" Why do you say those things about him?

So many people tell me "It hurts too much to think about him" after a pet dies. That's true, but only partially. I think everyone whose pet has died can remember at least one incident he shared with the animal that will make him laugh at the memory—laughter that's inevitably mixed with tears. Pets provide their owners with vicarious pleasures. You may have enjoyed watching your dog get to know strange new things as a puppy, or shun a frivolous toy with the dignity of age, or watch your cat step into snow for the first time. Perhaps you marvel, even now, at your pet's peculiar preferences for sleeping and eating at odd hours or in bizarre places. The pleasure you found in his company is only somewhat diminished when he dies because no one can take your memories away. What's more, that recalled joy acknowledges the animal's value in your life—a value that automatically justifies the length and depth of your sorrowful reactions to his death. Think of those intimate memories if it worries you to grieve for a beloved animal. When someone says "It was only a pet" you'll know that's not true. If you can define what that animal was in your life and what he stood for, you can say to yourself "No, he wasn't just an animal. He was the family clown," or "my best friend," or "an unabashed pumpkin-bread thief," or "a walking reminder of my father."

You may come up with several different definitions for that pet, and each has its own value. I think few relate to their pets in just one way because over time they go through so many experiences and emotions with them. Look at the categories that follow and think about those that best fit your relationship. Once you consider the characteristics that made him special you'll be better able to see why you grieve and mourn his death. It's not enough to say he was your companion—you need to figure out *what* kind of companion he was to face your bereavement effectively and to properly adjust to life without him.

"My Animals Became My Security Blankets"

Many people justify pet ownership by citing their need for protection, whether they live in an isolated rural area or a busy urban neighborhood. Cat owners jokingly refer to their "attack cats" while dog owners choose canines for their loud barks or their intimidating size. And almost anyone who owns a pet, whether for protection or pleasure, has probably wakened in the middle of the night and felt better knowing the animal was inside the house or just outside the door. That's true whether you live alone or with other people; a pet's presence ensures that at least one other being is with you in case of emergency. A phone by your bed, an alarm system, or watchful neighbors may provide the same sense of safety, but pets do more than ward off intruders. Your animal gives you emotional security as well, and that reliable gift may outweigh any physical protection he provides.

You might have first experienced that sense of security from a pet with whom you shared childhood or adolescence. When even your parents couldn't understand or comfort you, when no one else would listen to or stay with you, you could always count on the family pet. Marylou, a twenty-three-year-old woman with a child of her own, recalled the influence her childhood pets had: "Because I was an only child, and my father was away at sea most of the time, my animals became my security blankets," she said. "They were there when I laughed, when I cried, and when I simply needed someone to talk to about things I couldn't tell anyone else."

It's those reliable qualities in pets that also boost morale and ensure well-being. Pets don't argue with you. They pay attention to your slightest glance, to your affectionate hugs, and to your most secret confessions. They can't interrupt, contradict, or betray you. Sometimes children in a multiple-pet household create particular alliances with different pets, counting on the animals to ensure support in any argument—and confirmation that they have a friend who reinforces their feelings. Owners far older and wiser also design roles for their pets that help them cope with daily life. It's natural for either a child or an adult to take comfort in the reliability of a pet's presence. A single adult never has to come home and be alone or lonely if a pet's there; a mother who works at home can delay loneliness when her children leave if an animal remains in the house. Couples who argue may take sides with the pets, as children sometimes do. If you're going through a divorce the pet you owned before the marriage can be counted on to see you through to its end. Because he knew you when you were single he may remind you that when the divorce takes place you'll be able to survive.

You're never too old to value that emotional safety and silent, consistent support from your pet. He becomes a sort of sanctuary for you after an argument or a stressful day at work, when your friends forget you or your spouse dies, when no words can comfort you or you just need someone to talk to. Because he gives without demanding much in return, you can easily consider him among the best of your friends and a secure companion.

"He Needs Me": Pets as Children

You may never speak in baby talk to your animal or refer to a pet as your baby, although many do. But that doesn't stop your pet from representing, on an unconscious level, a child who cannot mature. He retains childlike qualities because he can never be completely self-sufficient; a pet will never completely be able to fend for himself in a house designed for human use. What's more, his needs are basic and similar to those of children—food, shelter, medical care, protection, sleep —so it's natural for you to value and appreciate your pet's dependency on you. Every owner can say "He needs me" with conviction.

You may find you rely on that dependency even more as you grow older. Nancy found that true when her youngest son departed for a college two thousand miles from home. She was fifty-five when he started his freshman year, and her husband still had ten years to work before retirement. "I had no desire to put myself through the enormous effort of finding a job just to keep busy," she said. "We didn't need extra money, although Jack couldn't retire early because of Tommy's tuition. I wasn't about to travel without my husband, and I didn't want to sit around watching soap operas, either. Tommy was too far away to visit us often, and sometimes he preferred to spend his breaks with kids from school. But I found out pretty quickly that, even without kids around, I couldn't wallow in loneliness—the dog needed me." She told me a story that's common to many women in similar situations: Shep, the family collie, didn't actively demand her attention, he simply followed Nancy around the house, moving from room to room as she cleaned and as the sun moved, looking for a warm spot in which to nap. She fixed him meals when she made her own and took him with her to get the mail or to run errands at a neighborhood store. She came to depend on his companionship, much as she'd unconsciously relied on her children's presence in previous years.

"My husband went through the same process too," Nancy said, "although we never talked about it until Shep died. He said he'd miss coming home from work the most. Even though none of the kids were around to yell 'Dad's home! When do we eat?' the dog would greet him at the door. Shep had even helped us talk to Tommy, in a way—even when Tommy didn't care to hear what *we* were doing, he wanted an update on the dog."

Other people see a pet's resemblance to a child more clearly. "Brandy was the child I never wanted to have," wrote Carla, a Texas woman. "I didn't want or need a baby, because she was enough to fulfill my need to love something or somebody." Again, considering a pet to be your only child isn't necessarily strange, due to the animal's immature and dependent nature. Everyone needs to be needed, and you can expect to turn to an animal for fulfillment since he'll rely on you as long as he lives. I think it's difficult to determine when this perception grows out of control. No pet can substitute completely and constantly for human relationships, but he can supplement or substitute for them temporarily when they falter, end, or change. As long as you realize that, you can enjoy your pet's childlike qualities without hesitation.

"He Remembers Me as I Was"

You may be a person who can proudly say "I've always owned animals" and mean it—from earliest infancy to your own death, you may constantly live in the presence of at least one pet. Or you may look back to discover you've had only one stint as a pet owner but that those years coincided with an important transition: from single to married, unemployed to employed, child to adult, married to divorced or widowed, poor to rich, or simply confused to calm. Whatever the situation, you probably take comfort in the pet who knew you during a particularly happy or difficult stage in your life. Because that animal went through changes with you, he has added value now. You may have shared the experience with him, perhaps confiding your feelings. He may have helped you through a rough transition or joined your celebrations during a happy time. Best of all, he reminds you of how you've changed over the years, bridging the gap between past and present.

Barry, a thirty-year-old financial analyst living in New York City, remembers his cat, Horatio, as the measure of his first successes in the working world. "I even named him for those Horatio Alger stories, the ones that say you can make it if you work hard," Barry recalled. "When I found Horatio in the alley next to my apartment building, he looked as down on his luck as I was—that was our common bond." As Barry looked for work, making endless phone calls and sitting through unsuccessful interviews, the cat shared his trials and tribulations. "We literally almost starved together. Skinny cat, skinny owner, you know?" Barry said. "When I finally landed a job, we celebrated. Both of us enjoyed the regular pay—Horatio was getting tired of eating spaghetti with ketchup on it instead of sauce, when he really only wanted cat food." Horatio and Barry had become so close during those hard times that the cat heard many of his owner's worries and hopes over the years that followed. He saw Barry through a job switch, broken-off relationships, promotions, an engagement, and his marriage's early years. "Just his name reminded me not to get too complacent, not to forget how hard we'd worked in those first few years— and I feel as if we came through it together, as a team," Barry said. "So it really shocked me when he died. I was someone else entirely. I had a wife, I had the position of the guy who first hired me. When Horatio died no one else was left who remembered me as I was way back when, and that's a sobering thought."

Practically speaking, Horatio was one of the few constant factors in Barry's rapidly changing life. Pleasure and reassurance came from a companionship based on shared experiences, as many people find with college roommates, siblings, office associates, and other peers who know where they've been and where they're headed. But again, because a pet is so much more available as a constant presence, that sharing can be almost as complete as with any human friend. You may have a busy job and a full social schedule as a single, but when you come home alone your animal's with you. In your childhood the pet saw you with your family at the dinner table and by yourself, hiding in your bedroom. A retired person's pet watches visitors and delivery people come and go, but remains with his owner when no one comes to the house to visit. As a result you may feel better able to handle setbacks and difficult transitions because your pet is always there.

Most owners react as Meg did—with gratitude and praise—when a pet provides them with crucial support and perspective during a troublesome era. "I went through two miscarriages before I had my beautiful daughter," wrote Gail, a thirty-five-year-old from Iowa. "And Charlie, my golden retriever, treated me no differently—he was always there, in pleasure or in pain, so I could hug him, cry with him, be happy with him. If he hadn't been around, I don't know whether I'd have been able to keep going." Dan, a professor at a small Virginia college, went through three degree programs with his beagle, Buckaroo. "Buck went to the University of California, Cornell, and Harvard, and even did some summer sessions with me at Ball State," he wrote. "We went through so much together I always said he could take over my classes when I was sick!" And Jennifer, a twenty-five-year-old account executive at an advertising agency in New York, told me that "when my boss was too distant, my co-workers too competitive, and the pressure hit the breaking point, the only thing that kept me going was Romanoff, my tabby. I'd hold her close and cry at night, sitting on my living-room floor. And then she'd cajole me into some kind of game, forcing me to forget those problems for a while."

Again, it's important to remember you owe yourself much credit and gratitude for dealing with major life transitions. That doesn't diminish, though, the contributions your pet made to your comfort during that era in your life—or the pain and insecurity you may feel once he's gone.

"He Means Everything to Me"

As you read through this section you may realize that all the relationships described here apply to you and your pet. That's true of Meg, who found emotional security, an outlet for caring, and an important aid through troubled times in Gypsy. But one particular type of owner more often combines all those levels of friendship and affection with a pet, ultimately considering the animal his reason for being—the owner who has suffered multiple losses of various kinds, feeling as a result that life isn't worth living except for the pet's sake.

This almost sums up Meg's relationship with Gypsy, although the losses she dealt with at a young age were unusual. It's far more common for an aged pet owner to see an animal as the sole inspiration to continue living. Although that's a natural and normal relationship, many people belittle it. I've heard people scoff at an elderly person's dependency on a pet, as if it were a sign of senility. But few detractors consider how that person-pet relationship came to be and why it serves a valuable purpose.

If you're an older pet owner who lives alone with your animal, you experience many situations others don't face. You've gone through and can expect multiple types and levels of loss: your career, through voluntary or mandatory retirement; your friends and peers, through death or disability; your own mobility and health, through aging. You may find it difficult to visit others if you can no longer drive or walk great distances. Your children are less likely to visit you often since our mobile society may prompt them to move far away from you. The simplest motions or skills may elude you—as sight, hearing, speech, and movement diminish. Those losses may confine you to a smaller geographical area or even to your home and may limit your sources for caring as well. To some extent you may lose your motivation for living as full a life as you once did. Those things that spurred you to action every morning may no longer exist. An animal takes on a crucial role in your existence, making you feel needed and wanted.

Just as pets never lose their dependency on humans, you never lose the need for social relationships. That's why so many pet owners say that a pet "means everything to me." Humans sometimes determine their worth at least partially by their interactions with other creatures, human or animal. Furthermore, you need consistent companionship—more than contact with store clerks, delivery people, or a weekly bridge club. It's unfortunate that few resources exist to provide constant relationships for older people who live alone, if they want them. A pet may be the only companion available to you on an everyday basis. It's nobody's business, however, to say whether you should or should not own a pet for those reasons. A pet allows you to structure days that might otherwise seem aimless; he lets you talk, laugh, be physically affectionate and playful. You probably don't want to give those things up, and a pet may help you continue them.

It's important for those who haven't yet experienced this situation to remember that pets bring these benefits to older people only if they're welcome—animals have no magic qualities that can outweigh someone's dislike of pets. And even if the animal is wanted, he can't substitute entirely for human relationships.

"Dusty Was His Link with Dad"

You may have already experienced grief for a beloved person in your life before you go through it for your pet. A friend may have moved away or a family member may have died. It's possible your dog or cat helped you through that grief by reminding you of the person you lost, prompting pleasant and painful memories of past experiences shared with both the person and the pet. You may have owned the animal together, as a couple, or as a family; perhaps the person who died gave the pet to you. No matter which situation is yours, that animal stalls complete acceptance of the death simply by serving as a living reminder. He's even more precious to you, both for his own character and for the person he represents.

Jill, for example, was the youngest child of a man who hunted in his spare time with the family beagle, Dusty. "Everyone loved that dog," she recalled, "and he was even born on my birthday. My brother teased me a lot, saying we were twins. But Dusty was my father's dog more than anyone else's—when he got older and crankier, he'd let only me and my father come near him. And finally only Dad could feed or walk him."

When Jill was nineteen she and her family learned that her father was dying of cancer; he had less than six months to live. "My brother and I flew home from opposite sides of the country," she said. "By that time Dusty was seventeen years old and still devoted to Dad. Mom had her hands full taking care of Dad, and she didn't think Dusty would survive another Massachusetts winter. So my brother, Ron, took the dog with him to California when he went back. Supposedly, he did it for the dog's sake, for the warmer climate. But I could tell that he had more trouble than any of us dealing with Dad's cancer. Dusty was his link to Dad; he must have been Ron's only comfort when Dad died the following March. But Ron was even more devastated when the dog died two months after that."

Jill, even in her absence from the dog and her family, took comfort in knowing her brother could find the help he needed in the dog they'd once shared; her brother was able to care for Dusty in his last months as he couldn't his dying father. Both of them saw Dusty as a reminder of their father, remembering times when both were healthier and more active. Had Dusty lived longer he might have seen Ron through a long period of grieving for his father. In the same way, any animal that witnesses your life with someone can be evidence of your ability to survive, and can fill in for the person you miss so much until you're able to enjoy life again.

How Reminiscing Puts the Death in Perspective

Perhaps you've already gained some insights about why you may grieve so deeply for a pet when he dies. Your pet's death takes away the benefits you unconsciously enjoyed—the emotional security, companionship, guarantees against loneliness, fulfillment of your need to be needed. If your pet served as a reminder of a person you've lost, you must come to grips with a dual bereavement, finally accepting both losses. The animal that helped you move from one era to the next now completes that rite of passage with his death; as Barry pointed out, you may see yourself as a different person, grown out of the habits and characteristics you had when you first owned the pet.

For those reasons, and many others, you may feel temporarily out of control just because your pet was such a reliable, constant presence. His familiar habits, good or bad, let you know what to expect; now you may resist for a while continuing your life without that comfortable set of known experiences. If your pet was your primary source of companionship, you may not want to risk another one just yet. And if your pet served as a permanent anchor for your emotions and reactions, you can easily feel as if you now lack crucial support for your pain.

Each of those types of relationships with pets, and their termination through a pet's death, can determine whether, and for how long, you'll feel guilty, angry, depressed, or unwilling to accept the death. Feelings of sorrow are the last part of the social system behavior described earlier in this chapter—*natural results of your relationship with a pet.* Just as it's normal to fall into patterns of response to your pet and the people around you, it's normal to react with painful and puzzling feelings when those interactions come to a halt. I hope you can see that more than just a pet has died by reminiscing about what your animal meant to you, what he provided, and what you gave to him. Of course you shouldn't spend the rest of your life haunted by these memories, but I think you *should* use those remembered antics, habits, and special reminiscences to convince yourself your grief is valid and justified. Thinking about your past with this pet may show you aspects of the relationship you never noticed, positive discoveries that may surprise and please you. No one can tell you why that relationship had to end, but you can figure out for yourself why it hurts so much to lose it. It's up to you to define why your pet was so special. No one else can be responsible for this vital step toward your recovery— and no other person, ultimately, can take that definition, or its meaning, away.

3
Your Reactions to Choosing Euthanasia

"In all my sixty-eight years of living a full life, I've had dark days, but yesterday was the darkest. I'm heartbroken because of the deep feeling of loss, but I'm also overwhelmed with an unbearable guilt because of the impulsive manner in which I made this decision. . . . I hugged and kissed Ernie several times, told him I loved him, and then broke down and left. When I got home I called to say I changed my mind, but it was too late."

As I make my regular morning rounds at the hospital with a cup of coffee to accompany me, I talk to the nurses and clinicians to uncover any concerns they may have for their patients' owners. One morning Dr. Jim Barnes was waiting for me, eager to discuss one of the previous night's cases referred from the emergency service. The case was difficult medically, but he seemed more concerned about the owner's anxiety.

Wilfie, a small Cairn terrier, had had a kidney problem confirmed overnight; additional information about his condition was sketchy. His owner, Janine, had gone home when Wilfie was hospitalized at 10 P.M., but she'd called the emergency service every hour until 3 A.M. That morning she arrived when the building opened at seven o'clock.

I suggested to Dr. Barnes that we both go to see her. If she seemed willing I'd spend some time talking with her while he developed a tentative treatment plan for Wilfie. Janine looked both tired and nervous when we met her in the reception area. "How is he?" were her first words. After Dr. Barnes told her the dog seemed stable, and left, I explained my role at the hospital and mentioned our concern for her. At that point she broke down. "Wilfie's all I have left!" she sobbed. I let her cry for a while, brought her a cup of coffee, and then asked her to tell me all about her dog.

Wilfie's importance quickly became clear. For the past eight months Janine's life had been a nightmare. She'd returned to school in the fall to finish a master's degree in psychology, work she had delayed because of her son's birth five years earlier. A routine school physical suggested she might have some abnormalities; further tests confirmed she was in the early stages of multiple sclerosis. Shortly thereafter, her husband and son were killed simultaneously in a holiday automobile accident.

She described Wilfie this way: "He's always been special. My husband gave him to me for a birthday present about eight years ago, and we did all sorts of things together. After my son was born, Wilfie took care of him. They were such pals, always wrestling and chasing each other.

"After the accident I don't think I'd have made it without Wilfie there. He always listened to my sorrow, my anger, whatever I was feeling. I never had to be alone. Wilfie and I just had each other. If I have to lose him, too, I don't know if I can handle it. This may seem kind of silly, but what will I do?"

By this time Dr. Barnes had been gone for thirty-five minutes, so I excused myself and went to find him. Wilfie was in the final stages of kidney failure, he reported, and would probably die within a couple of months, perhaps sooner.

We agreed two things were critical: Janine needed to know the truth immediately, and I needed as much time as possible to help her prepare herself for Wilfie's inevitable death.

After Dr. Barnes explained Wilfie's condition, Janine's silence was devastating. Her face was drawn with pain, showing all her stress and hopelessness. Finally, she asked what she should do. The three of us reviewed the options, finding two realistic choices: she could authorize euthanasia or try to make Wilfie as comfortable as possible at home. Janine told us she knew euthanasia was sensible, but she couldn't bring herself to let go so quickly—Wilfie really *was* the last surviving member of her family, and besides, he didn't look all that sick. It seemed perfectly reasonable to let her be somewhat selfish, to hang on to Wilfie, and to think of her own needs. I told her I was confident she'd know when the dog's needs had to be met.

Two days later Janine and Wilfie were back. "I can't see him continue to suffer on my account," she said. "He's been too special to me. He deserves to die the way he lived, with dignity."

Her decision wasn't as sudden as it may seem; we'd spent many hours in those two days talking about Wilfie and how much his presence in the past year had helped her. She doubted, cried, and felt angry and sad by turns, but Janine took time to express her feelings. She came to accept how much she and the dog had given one another, and she drew inner strength from their bond. Choosing euthanasia would hurt her as much as it would sustain Wilfie's dignity, but she chose it as the best option for both of them. Now Janine has her degree, a new job, and a more courageous outlook on life—all of which she credits to Wilfie and the time we spent dealing with his death.

Janine was fortunate. She had detailed medical advice, emotional support, and the encouragement to talk about her despair and dread before she made her decision. She also knew the choices were hers—including the choice to keep Wilfie alive as long as possible. But every day thousands of pet owners make that same decision without taking time to consider how they'll react to it later—mainly because they lack any warning or support for what's to come. They select humane death for their beloved pets to eliminate pain and suffering, yet nobody acknowledges how much emotional pain they themselves will experience.

Bill was just one of many people who found out how euthanasia would affect him only after he chose it for his wire-haired terrier, Ernie. The realization hit him so swiftly and strongly he poured out his feelings in a letter written to me within twenty-four hours of Ernie's death. "In all my sixty-eight years of living a full life, I've had dark days," Bill wrote, "but yesterday was the darkest. I'm heartbroken because of the deep feeling of loss, but I'm also overwhelmed with an unbearable guilt because of the impulsive manner in which I made this decision, so critical to my happiness and self-esteem."

In pages of labored writing, with no detail omitted, Bill described Ernie's complicated medical history. Ernie, he told me, was sixteen years old. He'd had a rectal tumor for several years, as well as chronic ear infections, anal discharges, bleeding gums, warts, arthritis, and a 90 decibel hearing loss. When he chose to lie down somewhere he could rise only with great difficulty and pain; as a result, the dog spent most of each day sleeping in one place. What's more, he was incontinent—so much so that Bill and his wife finally had to lock Ernie out of their bedroom, where he'd slept at the foot of the bed for the past fifteen years. Walking, running, and jumping onto the patio couch for a quick nap had been Ernie's favorite pastimes, Bill wrote, but pain had curtailed almost all activity by now. Pausing from the list of medical problems, Bill reminisced briefly about his pleasure with Ernie during the dog's healthy years. "He was my constant companion," he wrote, "and I enjoyed our long walks most of all. In his early years Ernie compelled me to walk at set times during the day. He helped me to establish what has become a lifetime habit of regular walks."

Because he received sheer happiness from his active pet, Bill gave back every moment of pleasure in devotion to his now-ailing animal. He did what he could to make Ernie comfortable at home; then, when the tumor began to bleed, he consulted the veterinarian who'd treated Ernie since he'd been a pup. On examination the tumor turned out to be untreatable. It would probably continue to bleed sporadically, and even corrective surgery wouldn't help much—in fact, the tumor might never heal if the surgery were performed. The veterinarian delivered his prognosis, adding, "I'm afraid there's nothing else we can do." Bill decided right then that euthanasia was his only option.

"I hugged and kissed Ernie several times, told him I loved him, and then broke down and left," wrote Bill of his "impulsive" decision. "When I got home I called to say I had changed my mind, but it was too late."

Just one day later Bill was "fairly bursting with regrets" and ready to reveal them. "I wish I had gone to another doctor for a second opinion. I wish I had given Ernie a good grooming and a big meal of his favorite food. Most of all, I wish I had decided to get him through another spring and summer, at least. I even miss getting up during the night to let him go outside to relieve himself; I miss being alert to any sign of his need to go out during the day. I miss giving him his medication; washing his eyes and ears; treating his rectum; washing, brushing, and grooming his coat. Recently it became too inconvenient to take him with us on trips and, in the last month, almost impossible to leave him alone for any length of time. But now that we're free to travel, I feel too guilty to go anywhere. I can't enjoy my golf, my new car, or even eating a good meal.

"For the first time in my life," Bill wrote, "I'm less reluctant to die because I look forward to seeing Ernie again. I know how unrealistic it is to expect a reunion with my pet, but I can't seem to stop mourning. Please help me."

My first message to Bill was, "I wish your circumstances had been different." I wasn't referring to the way Ernie died, but to the situation that caused Bill to think of his choice as "the biggest mistake of my life." He'd had the medical information he needed to make the decision, as Janine had, but he lacked the two resources she'd found in our staff: encouragement to think about the choices over time, and people receptive to hearing her thoughts. With that support Bill might have chosen euthanasia with more awareness of its impact, and without so many regrets. Instead, he felt only shame—when the real shame was that no one had said something like "I imagine you must feel terrible about Ernie's condition. Yes, euthanasia is one option, but because he won't die immediately, you can still take him home and care for him for a while longer. We both know he'll continue to fail; he probably won't live much longer. But why don't you think it over? Take Ernie home for a few days; then call me if you have any doubts or questions. When you're ready we can discuss the process in more detail."

Those words would have at least cushioned the blow, helping Bill prepare for those painful decisions and acknowledging his unspoken wish to make them with as much care and thought as he'd given Ernie all those years. Bill might have gone home after that conversation to find another veterinarian's opinion, but that seems unlikely. He'd probably have spent many hours with Ernie, coming to grips with the thought of his death, talking to him, preparing that last fancy meal and grooming him meticulously. He might have returned to the veterinarian two days later, as Janine did, convinced euthanasia was not just necessary but *right*—for his sake and for Ernie's.

Or those words might have spurred him to act as he did, authorizing euthanasia without delay. No matter when he acted it would have been impossible to think of his choice as reckless or rash. I pointed out to Bill that he'd had at least one year of unconscious preparation for Ernie's death. The thought process described in his letter was long and laborious, not offhand and spontaneous. After he'd cared so diligently for Ernie, hour after hour, day after day, something inside Bill must have told him that his efforts to keep Ernie alive had become unreasonable—that it was unfair to him and to Ernie to go on that way. He knew their relationship had shifted from joyful companionship to worried guardianship—that

Ernie might have been alive but wasn't himself anymore. He probably needed only to hear someone say "Yes, it's okay to do this as long as you realize how difficult the choice is, and how you'll feel about it later."

When you choose euthanasia for your pet you face the same reactions other bereaved pet owners confront: denial, anger, guilt, and depression. But because this humane death is your choice, an unusual role and responsibility can magnify those feelings and add other emotions to your bereavement. To prepare for them you must first understand the process you're considering. You may choose euthanasia for a variety of reasons, so we'll look at some special situations to show you the highly different needs that may convince you to consider euthanasia for your pet.

What Happens When "There's Nothing More We Can Do"

Euthanasia evokes such painful images that few pet owners initiate the conversation about this option. You may have an impression or hunch that euthanasia should or will be considered if your pet is extremely ill, old, or injured; in other cases, when medical problems are slow to develop or less visible, the option may come as a complete surprise. In any case you'll probably hear your veterinarian say something similar to "There's nothing more we can do for your pet." He will most likely lead up to or follow that statement with reasons: prohibitive costs of treatment, levels of pain the pet will experience, ineffectiveness of treatment, or simply a lack of understanding about fighting your animal's uncommon disease. If your pet has been hurt in an accident, it may be the damage is too widespread and severe to allow rehabilitation. But if your veterinarian doesn't volunteer specific information, ask him to explain. I'm not suggesting you mistrust him or the information he provides; instead, you need to know why nothing else can be done for your pet so you can understand what's happening and prepare yourself for your subsequent decisions and reactions.

Once you know why your pet's health appears to be beyond help, and understand any test or examination results that confirm his condition, you should listen carefully while your veterinarian reviews your options. Generally speaking, it's neither the veterinarian's role nor his responsibility to recommend euthanasia over further treatment, or vice versa. He should tell you that three basic choices are available: euthanasia, to eliminate further suffering by putting the pet to death quickly and painlessly; treatment or medication, to potentially delay death and make his condition more tolerable; or neither. The last choice allows you to take your animal home until he dies of his ailment or to seek an opinion from another veterinarian. Don't feel foolish about asking for any of the options that fall short of euthanasia; it's important you feel you've done *everything possible, within reason,* before you consider humane death for your pet. Although you should seek and rely on your veterinarian's assessment, he can't make these decisions for you. He may encourage you to find out more about your pet's condition and his chances for recovery. When eighteen-year-old Tina brought her cat, Marvin, into the VHUP emergency service late one night after a car accident, she said, "I pretty much knew what the outcome would be even before we got to the hospital. At first, though, I felt like a fool, crying in front of all those doctors. But Dr. Anderson made it clear it was okay to cry. When I hesitated to have them waken another doctor to receive a second opinion, even though they suggested it, she said right away that if it were her cat, she'd certainly seek everything available. That's how I felt, but it was so reassuring to hear they thought it was okay too."

For each option—further treatment, euthanasia, or neither—your veterinarian should explain these details:

Procedure.   Exactly what will and will not be done to your pet? Who will conduct tests, operate, prescribe medications? Can you be present? When will you know the results of tests or surgery? How long will the process take? Must you sign a release form? Is your veterinarian willing to meet with you after these procedures to discuss their success or failure?

Expected Effect.   Is there any reasonable chance of cure? If so, will it be complete? If not, how much additional time might treatment give your pet before he dies? What will the quality of that extra time be—painful or comfortable? Will he be better able to function? Will your pet have to stay in the hospital for a long time? What will the procedure eliminate—pain, disability, further deterioration? What will it cause—side effects, potential death, improved condition? Will it make a difference?

Costs.   What will each test, operation, hospital stay, and prescribed medication cost, separately and totaled? How much does euthanasia cost? How much is the bill already? What is the hospital's payment policy?

You should be asking these questions of yourself as well as of the veterinarian and measuring them with yet another query: is the option worth it, considering all those factors? The point of this conversation with your pet's doctor is to receive enough information to make an intelligent, enlightened decision.

Understanding the Euthanasia Process

Before you make any decisions, however, you should find out exactly what will happen if you choose euthanasia. It's crucial that you clearly comprehend every aspect of the procedure. Toward that end no veterinarian should ever refer to euthanasia in a way that might confuse you. If your pet's doctor talks about "putting him to sleep," "putting him down," or "easing his misery," you should inquire whether he's referring to a sedative for sleep, a pain-reducing medication, or a humane death for your pet. I know it may be difficult for you to say those words, but you must understand what will happen to your pet before you give authorization for any procedure. It's not a stupid question; *many owners mistake these euphemisms for honest descriptions of short-term treatment options rather than irreversible death*. Your veterinarian shoud clarify his words; if you're unsure, as with any other option, ask him to explain.

Choosing euthanasia actually puts more decisions before you, most regarding your participation in the process. Veterinary euthanasia is generally the same all over the United States: a lethal dose of an injectable drug is given your pet, eliminating both life and pain in a matter of seconds. Although other euthanasia methods have been and may be used, this one is preferred and recommended by the American Veterinary Medical Association, the American Animal Hospital Association, and the clinicians themselves. You may, however, ask whether your veterinarian uses another procedure. If he does you should receive a full explanation of what will happen to your pet and find out whether this method has the approval of the veterinary profession.

It's difficult to say whether pet owners prefer this method, too, because you won't know exactly what the experience feels like until or unless you witness it. That's your first option: *do you want to be present?* Your veterinarian should offer you this option as a matter of course or agree to it at your suggestion. Many people find they can't bring themselves to watch; others won't authorize the procedure unless they're allowed to be present. The most appropriate choice will be the one with which you feel most comfortable. After witnessing many euthanasia injections with pet owners, I can tell you it always surprises me how quickly death follows the injection, and the owner is usually just as surprised. In seconds the animal appears to take one last breath, then remains still. The dog or cat looks no different, except he's neither breathing nor feeling the effects of disease or injury. If any pain is involved for the pet, it's a momentary twinge that occurs when the veterinarian inserts a needle into his vein—a feeling no different from all of the vaccinations and booster shots he's had over the years.

Your second option, whether you choose to watch the euthanasia or stay away, is *to spend some time alone with your pet before the injection is given*. Again, suggest this to your veterinarian if he doesn't mention it. It may be a good idea to take the opportunity to say goodbye to your pet, because euthanasia gives you enough control over the situation to do so. Had your pet died in his sleep, in an accident, or on an operating table, you might not have had that choice. You may prefer to say good-bye to him at home, allowing someone else to take him to the veterinary clinic. If you think being present during the euthanasia or just before it will upset you too much, you can always absent yourself. At no time should you be ashamed or embarrassed about making these choices, whatever you decide. Most pet owners feel torn between being present or absent, apprehensive that the injection will be painful to watch, yet wanting to stand by a faithful dog or cat until the end. You simply need to pay attention to your feelings and follow the strongest ones, the ones that will give you the most peace later on. Although this may be the kindest death for your pet, it's possibly the hardest thing you'll ever do, so it's worth careful consideration.

Your third option ties in with the other two: when can you schedule euthanasia? Again, this decision should be yours, perhaps with some advice from others. In most cases you'll have to schedule the procedure during your veterinary clinic's hours of operation. Beyond that restriction you don't necessarily have to agree to an inconvenient time. Only your pet's sudden, severe, and debilitating health problem might require you to decide on almost immediate euthanasia, and even in that infrequent instance the veterinarian should allow as much time as possible for you to prepare yourself. *Your* feelings and needs deserve high priority at this point, particularly if you wish to witness the process.

The Euthanasia Dilemma:
"Am I Doing the Right Thing?"

Monica almost qualified as a self-taught animal expert—her large collection of cats and dogs included many different breeds. She took pains to understand their medical care and special diets because they were both her pets and her working partners in a program she conducted for children who fear animals. She was realistic about death but found it particularly hard to handle two deaths in one month. First, her sixteen-year-old tomcat, Skipper, developed a degenerative bone disease so severe she elected euthanasia for him, with her veterinarian's support. Then, one month later, her fourteen-year-old schnauzer, Ricky, died of natural causes. "I agonized over Skipper's death, and took what seemed forever to recover," she told me. "But because I didn't have to make the decision to kill Ricky, I didn't have to worry about whether I'd done the right thing."

She was seeking my help a year after these deaths because she faced yet another: Tasha, her border collie, appeared to have a form of diabetes both difficult and expensive to treat. A previous stomach disorder may have inadvertently damaged the eight-year-old dog's kidneys as well. The combination of problems made Tasha's eating difficult and her constant intake of fluids necessary. "Because she takes in huge quantities of water, she has to urinate at least every four hours, day and night," Monica said, adding, "She also seems to have a low-grade chronic pain, because I can hear her moan occasionally. She still manages to eat some foods, carries her tail in a normal position, and plays ball once or twice a week. In other words, she's still *sort of* happy, and can function *fairly* well." But those observations didn't give Monica any hope—they just made her questions about euthanasia more difficult to ask.

"Is there any way to convince yourself that killing the animal is right? My mind accepts it but my heart sure doesn't. I don't want her to suffer, so the decision looks inevitable. But I'd rather not go through the several months of anguish I felt after Skipper was killed," she admitted.

Monica faced unusual and powerful decisions in this

case, complicated because of the previous euthanasia and natural death that had happened so close together and heightened by her better-than-average commitment to animal health care. But her questions were no different from those of any other pet owner considering euthanasia. Many seek me out to hear that humane death is acceptable; they want me to sanction the process they dread as well as their feelings about it. Many of them puzzle over the tug of war between emotions and logic, thinking such a struggle implies that euthanasia is bad or wrong.

Such confusion and doubt are natural results when you consider this unnatural yet humane act. Euthanasia is intended to relieve pain by hastening death in a caring way, yet it may leave you feeling uneasy. You may have always considered any kind of death as ugly, painful, and horrible—this one seems even more so because you control it. Most people find controlled deaths—such as murders and suicides—unacceptable. Euthanasia for people is still considered murder, at least in courts of law. Despite the good intentions behind the act, no one wants to take responsibility for a life that might continue without such a drastic step. The process is legal for pet animals because many people perceive them as helpless creatures, unable to care for themselves to the extent that humans or wild animals can. You may think, therefore, that a pet's struggle with a fatal illness or injury is particularly cruel and senseless. The dog or cat can't tell you his needs, desires, or feelings, nor can he solve this inevitable problem of living in pain; his approaching death makes him seem even less able to cope with his ailment. Such commitment to pets' inability to fend for themselves has been a strong part of many cultures and civilizations; in England and America those attitudes shaped the anti-cruelty laws, written first for animals and only later for human children.

With those contrasts between human strength and animal weakness in mind, you may find it difficult to grasp just why veterinary medicine can't always cure or protect your pet—particularly if he's always been, or seemed, healthy before. If humans are so much stronger and smarter than these creatures, why can't we stop their pain and prolong their lives? Veterinarians share these frustrations with you, although you may not know it. Most of them realize that even their extensive training and education can't solve every problem. One VHUP veterinarian, for example, handled a case I recall clearly because he spent as much time discussing his regrets with me as did the owners. The dog he treated was Toby, an eight-year-old mixed-breed who suffered severe rear leg fractures in an automobile accident. When his owners, the Morrisons, rushed him into the hospital emergency service, he went into cardiac arrest on the examination table. The veterinarian managed to revive the dog but sent him to the intensive care unit with little hope for his recovery. Toby, however, was tenacious; he improved enough in several weeks to go home with the Morrisons. One week after his discharge from the hospital, he was back. The repaired fractures had developed infections the Morrisons' private veterinarian could not treat successfully. Our clinician realized further surgery and treatment would neither stop the infections nor keep Toby alive. Offering euthanasia as an option to the Morrisons was a crushing blow to this doctor. He knew how unfair it would seem, how ill prepared they'd be for a euthanasia choice after that traumatic accident and Toby's apparently miraculous recovery because he thought it equally unfair and surprising. Just because he'd seen countless animals recover and others die didn't make him immune to feelings of confusion and frustration.

Once you accept the limits to veterinary medical care, even in the best facilities, you still face disturbing considerations. You almost have to worry, as Monica did, whether you're doing the appropriate thing—it's that natural a reaction. In addition you must confront a surprising discovery: the choice for euthanasia must be as appropriate for you as it will be for your pet because your feelings about the process during this time of consideration may well determine the extent of your reactions later.

"My Heart Can't Accept It": Your Needs

Many people realize euthanasia is a judgment call regarding a pet's quality of life. But before you consider that issue, I think you can help yourself by assessing *your* quality of life with your pet. Are you, like Bill, spending days and nights with all your senses alert only to your pet's needs, anticipating his pain, and attending to his disabilities? Think about the pattern of care you give him: have your regular duties not only increased but become inflexible? Might that routine become a long-standing one? Can your life with this ailing pet ever return to its original, enjoyable state? Or has it turned into a continual series of treatments, waiting, and apprehension? Do your efforts really help him—or do they help *you* more? That's the important consideration: are you being slightly selfish about delaying his inevitable death, just because you can't bear to part with him right now? If you can recognize and admit that feeling, then it's completely normal, acceptable, and understandable. Who wouldn't loathe and resist the prospect of losing such a valued friend when death approaches? It's natural to procrastinate when you have the option to end the relationship in this manner.

Bill, for example, knew deep down how much he cherished Ernie's company, even when the dog's condition deteriorated to its worst point. He wanted to follow those self-centered instincts but had no encouragement to see them as natural, forgivable, and appropriate to his situation. Janine felt fine about considering herself first, and had our support to act on those feelings when Wilfie's impending death came as such a shock. And Monica anticipated that her needs would mean as much as Tasha's did, expressing it beautifully: her mind, she said, could accept the dog's euthanasia. Her heart could not, because her heart's desire was to keep Tasha with her as long as possible.

It may be easier for you to accept your preferences as important if you realize they won't be the sole basis for your eventual decision. If most pet owners chose euthanasia strictly to fulfill their own needs, few would choose it for their animals. You'll of course consider your pet's needs as well as your own, helping to balance what may seem terribly callous self-concern. Euthanasia is a process with great tragedy built in: your choice helps your pet as it tears you apart emotionally. By claiming the right to consider your own needs, if that seems necessary, you'll anticipate the hurt you may feel and acknowledge you need time to prepare for the loss you'll experience.

I'm not sure anyone can choose euthanasia without some doubt and heartache when the pet in question is a special one. But I know the decision-making process not only allows for, but requires, your feelings. Don't stop your considerations with that selfish twinge—*look ahead*, no matter how apprehensive you may be, at how you'll feel after your pet dies by your own choice. What emotions fill your thoughts? What might the death mean to you? Will you be able to remember parts of the process with some satisfaction or contentment? Perhaps the greatest paradox intrinsic to euthanasia is that many owners eventually see it as a selfless decision. They sometimes consider it the ultimate commitment they can make to their special companions when no other viable option exists. That perspective will be easier to accept if you prepare for your reactions in advance.

Eliminating Pain: "My Pet Deserves This Death"

So many people ask me, or a veterinarian, or both of us, to decide for them. When you consider your pet's quality of life, it seems only natural to rely on professional advice. But there's still another limit to what a professional can contribute to this part of your decision. The veterinarian can report your pet's quality of health, an assessment that may include estimates of your pet's pain or difficulty, his longevity, and the effectiveness of treatments or medications. But only you can determine the quality of his life—which includes not only his health, but his happiness, habits, pleasures, and troubles.

That's exactly what I told Monica when she approached me with her indecision about euthanasia for Tasha. She told me immediately how the dog seemed to be: sort of happy, fairly functional, occasionally in pain. Her veterinarian had filled in other details, including the prospect of expensive and tedious treatments, eating problems, and fatigue. Monica had begun by deciding that Tasha's working days were over. Her constant need to urinate and periodic discomfort would keep the border collie away from the training she'd participated in for seven years.

All those facts were both inevitable and clear. Monica was juggling more difficult factors, consciously or unconsciously, and they were the same ones I hope you'll consider in this situation. Think of how your pet will feel if you keep him alive as long as possible; consider his current level of pain and the likelihood of increased pain in the months to come. You should also determine whether you'll be able to make him comfortable at home, from practical and medical standpoints. But the most decisive consideration of all may be whether your dog or cat is still struggling or willing to live.

Monica, for instance, had to think about Tasha: would the dog's pain and discomfort allow her to continue enjoying her life, even without work? Would she see her dog as the same being, or as a lesser, pained version of the pet she'd known and loved so long? For your own peace of mind you must feel as if you know your pet well enough by now to decide what he might want. You'll never really know whether he wants to live or die, give up or keep trying, but you're the person most capable of reasonably assessing those issues. How would you compare this situation to a previous experience with your dog or cat? Perhaps he's been through a similar problem and fought all the way through it, so he might want that chance again. Or perhaps not—this illness or injury may not be comparable for a variety of reasons. Some people may think it's silly to try to think as a pet would, but others strongly believe animals have a fighting instinct—one that tells them when to continue struggling to live. Wild animals, for instance, sometimes appear to give up life knowingly when they wander to a solitary spot to die. The looks and one-sided conversations you've had with your pet may now take on added significance as you try to gauge his viewpoint: one pleading, helpless look might be an unmistakable message that he wants to end this pain—or that he wants to keep on living.

No matter how you interpret your pet's feelings, you have to consider whether the nature of your relationship has changed and whether both of you can live with the altered friendship. Bill, for instance, knew Ernie might have stopped enjoying himself when he could no longer walk and run as he used to. He might have stood by the couch or slept at the door, looking as if he wanted to continue his old activities—an action that might have persuaded Bill of his discontent. Or it may have proven Ernie's desire to keep living. In this decision, where you are the unwilling judge and jury, you almost have to play attorney, too, building every case for your pet before you weigh the evidence. Each pet owner has a barometer or measure for his animal's quality of life, one connected to his feelings for the pet. Some people, faced with Ernie's incontinence, would have reacted by saying "He must feel so embarrassed, messing the carpets all the time—and sad, too, since we just can't let him sleep in the bedroom anymore. He can't help it, and that makes him feel awful. Let's not put him through this any longer." Perhaps they'd say "We can always get new rugs, but there'll never be another Ernie." Or, as Bill seemed to say, "Let's just cope. He's probably embarrassed, but he knows we love him no matter what. We'll do everything we can to help him cope."

It's most helpful simply to trust your own judgment on this, as I told Monica. If she felt euthanasia would be acceptable to herself and to Tasha, then it would be "the appropriate thing to do." Perhaps you'll have more confidence in your ability to make that decision when you look back at what you've done for the cat or dog throughout your life together. If you feel you've always done your best for your pet, I find it hard to believe you'd make an inappropriate, impulsive, or wrong choice on such a critical matter. I hope, in the end, you're able to say something similar to Janine's words: "He deserves to die as he lived, with dignity." Or happiness, or good health, or his wits about him. Whatever your measure, use it to gauge what you owe your pet as part of that special relationship and commitment before you make your decision.

How to Handle Anticipatory Grief

While you're considering euthanasia you may try to look ahead, imagining how you'll feel and what your life will be like without your pet. Sometimes that anticipation can seem so overwhelming that your fear actually takes control, preventing you from making any decisions at all, but that's rare. More often you begin to anticipate your feelings when you have made your choice for euthanasia. Guilt, denial, anger, or depression, or all four, come to you just as they would (and will) after the death, imitating the bereavement process even before your pet receives the injection that will end his life.

Just as those feelings vary in intensity and duration during actual bereavement, they may not follow any predetermined design during this anticipatory grief. This part of the emotional process is tentative; it allows you to try out your reactions now that you're sure your pet will die. In that sense it's helpful, and you can use this anticipation to express and acknowledge these emotions before they become a powerful bereavement experience. Sometimes the experience of anticipating grief can actually modify this later impact or at least give you a better sense of what to expect from yourself. That's not always the case, but it *can* happen.

But if any of these feelings seem overwhelming at this point—before the euthanasia—pay close attention to what is happening to you. You're likely to feel doubt and regret nag at your conscience; that's a natural response. You can also expect to feel relief, but don't be confused by it. You're not welcoming the thought that your pet will die but rather the success of having made a troubling, emotional decision. It may be dangerous, however, if you vehemently deny that your pet is dying, or fall into a deep depression, or grow angrier by the minute after you've decided on euthanasia. Subdued feelings—regret, doubt, self-concern—are common and expected before euthanasia. *Extreme* feelings are not. To immerse yourself so completely and intensely in emotions that still have no basis in fact will not help you. That anticipated set of reactions may or may not depict your actual feelings, and you'll need a true sense of your emotions in order to cope with the bereavement still to come. Should you feel those anticipatory feelings getting out of control, contact your veterinarian and arrange to delay euthanasia until you can better manage your reactions.

"Why Is It So Hard the Second Time?"

You've been through this before. Perhaps you were fortunate enough to have strong emotional support, an informative veterinarian's advice, and clearly presented options when you first chose euthanasia for a pet. You

know now, or know of, all the unknowns: what it feels
like, looks like, how you benefited from it, what decisions you face. You know you can get through it because you've done so at least once before.

Why didn't you feel this awful before? What's wrong
with you? *Something* must be wrong for you to feel
worse this time; the hard part, the first one, is over.
Why can't you bring yourself to make the decision or to
recover from the impact of the death as quickly as before?

Although it's natural to assume your previous experience with euthanasia may help you with a subsequent
decision, no two of these decisions are exactly alike.
Only the mechanics are common to each decision: the
discussion with the veterinarian, the consideration process, the actual decision, and witnessing or absenting
yourself from the injection. Beyond that, euthanasia
does *not* appear comparable to anything else in the
human experience, not even a previous similar decision.
I can't stress how startling, unusual, and personal this
decision always is by its very nature. So an attempt to
gauge your impending reactions based on your past experience probably won't succeed. The best result of
such comparisons is that you may well feel bad about
both decisions—guilty that the first was so much easier
to make and ashamed the next was so difficult, or vice
versa. Since the death will make you feel bad enough,
this is no time to add to your troubled emotions.

But it may help you to understand why these particular experiences are so disparate, why "it's so hard to
choose the second time," as many pet owners tell me.
You can do that by thinking about what went on between you and each pet for whom you considered euthanasia. Review what's happened in your life between

those decisions to change your perceptions, attitudes, and the nature of your relationships with pets and people. Perhaps the first pet was part of your family when life was more stable; you were younger, less worried, perhaps happier with your work. You might have had more available support from your family and friends, enough to absorb any shock or dismay you felt. If that's the case, as it was with Paula, you probably responded with less intensity. I spoke with Paula as she wavered over her second decision, ten years after the first. Bear, her giant black Newfoundland, was dying of cancer, painfully and slowly. Her feelings were complicated by his very identity: Bear had been a gift from Paula's mother, who'd died of cancer two years before. Her mother loved the dog as much as Paula did, and one of her last wishes was for her daughter to take special care of him. "I owe it to Mom," said Paula, shaking her head in confusion, "but I love Bear. He hurts, and nobody can stop that. I can barely keep up with what he needs —he's so large and yet so helpless now. And I don't think I can handle watching him go through everything Mom went through at the end, maybe because my memories of her are so tied up in his life as well as my own." Then she sighed and confessed something that really bothered her: "If I'd had my way, Mom would have had the option of euthanasia, but everyone was against it. I feel the same about Bear—but that would betray everything my mother did for me, and nobody would support me now if they didn't then. It wasn't this enormous a decision with our first dog—why is it all so tangled up now?"

Paula, in her nonstop rush of emotion, had laid out the reasons for herself, but it took time and many more discussions before she could grasp and accept them all.

It's fairly clear she had a far deeper emotional invest-
ment in Bear's life and well-being than in her other dog.
But Bear's disease was associated with her mother's,
and his death would be too. She cherished him as a gift
from her mother, and her return gift was that promise to
care for the dog. Her previous dog, however, had been
her husband's before they married. In Paula's life he
figured more as a household pet, and although she
shared in the euthanasia decision for him, she did so
without the level of difficulty she now experienced with
Bear.

And, as you might be, Paula was a changed person:
older, more thoughtful about life and death, and better
able to understand and appreciate the special aspects of
her relationship with Bear. Her first dog hadn't seemed
nearly as valuable and important to her life; Bear was
one of her best friends. In fact, many people find it
difficult to choose euthanasia the second time because
that next pet does seem more important and valuable as
a social companion and confidant. You may have spent
more time with him, understood his needs from a more
sensitive viewpoint, or dealt with personal issues con-
cerning his presence and companionship. Maybe he had
some silly habits or amusing rituals that cheered you
during the course of each day. All these considerations,
and many others as well, can precipitate new or different feelings and meanings about euthanasia for him.

It's easy to think you're going a little crazy—that
something might be wrong with your reaction to or your
feelings about this particular death and the decision to
make the death occur. That's often the case when you
didn't anticipate euthanasia for this second pet; if you're
caught off guard, you're apt to feel the response more
keenly. Again, your emotions don't follow strict guidelines; each instance is unique and variable. Try to avoid

expecting a specific reaction and realize no one can blame you for experiencing more *or* less hesitancy, doubt, or emotional upset.

"If He's Dying, Why Doesn't He Look Sick?"

You remember it clearly, although right now it seems ages ago: your cat had decided to attack your knitting basket for the umpteenth time, and at the moment you walked into the family room she was lying on her back in the midst of the biggest tangle of yarn you'd ever seen, rolling around as happily as if every strand were coated with catnip. While you told her in no uncertain terms that this was the last time she'd pull off her favorite trick, you noticed a funny lump on her side—your hand grazed it as you unwound her from the yarn.

Or maybe it was your last vacation day at the beach, and you had one final, raucous Frisbee game with your dog. He flew up and down the shoreline, dashing away from the waves as they rolled in, chomping on the plastic disc every time he caught it. But when you walked by his side on your way to the cottage later, you noticed his odd-sounding cough.

So now you're with your pet in the veterinarian's office. He's showing you printouts of the blood-test results, X rays, and other technical-looking charts you don't quite understand but his message is clear: your animal is riddled with tumors. He has a couple of months left, with luck, and he's probably fortunate the pain appears minimal. But yours isn't. To make matters worse, he's sitting there looking just as happy as he was yesterday.

If your pet has always been, or seemed, healthy, you're probably wondering what you got yourself into.

For once you decided to have that funny lump or cough checked out right away instead of waiting for it to pass. When your veterinarian confirms a fatal illness you may regret ever having sought his services. Ignorance may seem bliss to you at this point. At least you could have had more time to enjoy your pet's company without this awful fate hanging over your head. There's no way for you to adjust from playing with your seemingly healthy pet one day to choosing euthanasia for him the next without a great deal of ambivalence and inner turmoil.

Your surprise mixes doubt and denial, and you may find yourself demanding to know "How can I be sure you're right? How could this happen so fast? Why doesn't he *look* sick if he's getting ready to die?" If you can't see the signs of his illness, it's hard to believe the reality. You need tremendous trust in your veterinarian if your situation is similar, so listen carefully to what he tells you and ask as many questions as you can. Whether you choose euthanasia then, go home to consider the matter further, or decide to let your pet live out the time left to him, you must gather all the information *you* need to convince yourself the experience is indeed happening and your pet's death is not far off. Otherwise, you may face even greater anger and regret when your pet does die: you may berate yourself for failing to seek a second opinion, for not letting him live longer, or for letting him live too long. Remember, your impressions are often based on what you can see and what you want to hear; if your pet doesn't look sick or his life-threatening condition has come on swiftly, the decisions you make may be more complicated.

You should also be aware that this situation is most troublesome when you consider euthanasia a legitimate and humane option. All the usual convincing arguments in favor of humane death don't work as well in a case like this. Your pet's not in pain; you haven't had time to prepare; you may be afraid you can't handle waiting for his death to occur. What's more, neither you nor your veterinarian can know for sure when or whether the animal will begin to feel pain and discomfort if he continues to live. You need not choose euthanasia if you feel you can accept your pet's death when it comes naturally. Waiting until you can come to grips with the suddenness and shock of his impending death may be a better alternative, but the choice is up to you.

"I've Been This Route": Seriously Ill Owners

"Forget the chemotherapy," Pat snapped at her veterinarian. The clinician had been explaining her options for Taters, a ten-year-old mixed-breed dog. I looked at Pat carefully, waiting to see why she'd so quickly rejected this particular choice for Taters, who was dying of lymph node cancer. I didn't have to wait very long: it turned out Pat was dying from the same condition.

"Look," she said, trying to explain the intensity of her reaction. "Can you tell me it'll cure him? I know that lots of cancer research is done on dogs because the canine version is like the human version. But is it really going to buy him *time*? And if it does, just what *kind* of time will it be? Will he be better off than he is now, or is he going to lose his coat, vomit all the time, and be in even more pain? I suppose he'd have to spend half of his time here, too, during the treatments. I've gone this route myself, gentlemen. And if what happened to me is going to happen to Taters, forget it!"

It seems the most cruel of coincidences for both an owner and his pet to suffer the same serious illness because there's no escape for the owner. You suffer from your own pain and worry, well aware that your death may be approaching, and you see the same pain mirrored in one of your last remaining sources of happiness —your beloved animal. Although this coincidence might seem highly unusual, it's not rare in my experience. Owners like Pat have a keen awareness of treatment methods, side effects, and emotional adjustments to illness based on their own experience. They're more apt to seek help immediately. If you face this situation you may ask more complicated questions of your veterinarian and struggle with the euthanasia choice more than most others.

You should not feel as if you're the only person who's experiencing this double tragedy. A number of serious illnesses are common to both animals and humans—particularly carcinogenic and cardiac-related problems —and may be similar in terms of signs, pain levels, and treatment methods. The difference in life span between you and your pet also comes into play here: what seems like a childhood age to you is really an advanced age for your pet. Elderly animals are also prone to those diseases more likely to occur in older humans.

Although you can't help making comparisons in this situation, take care to avoid confusing your experience entirely with your animal's. Some differences do exist, and your veterinarian as well as your physician may be able to make them clear to you. The circumstance presents you with a very natural, normal vicarious experience. You may wonder whether you'll feel the same things and perhaps die in the same way your pet does. Those thoughts don't have to be a negative experience if they help prepare you for both deaths. As always, you must be aware of extreme reactions and monitor your own health with care even when you are more concerned about your animal. It's advisable, too, that you alert your personal physician, clergyman, or counselor to the situation. Although their specialties are not animal medicine, they need to understand your feelings and reactions as related to your pet's approaching death.

The most troublesome aspect again involves euthanasia, an option that's unavailable for you. You may choose it for your pet for exactly that reason, as Pat did. Consult as many reasonable sources of help as necessary to make your choices, and think the matter over carefully. With acknowledgment of the possibility of *both* your deaths, and a thorough search for the appropriate decision for your pet, you'll be able to handle this troubling turn of events to your advantage. If your pet's illness makes it easier for you to express your own fears and concerns about dying, then perhaps his death won't seem so pointless or damaging.

4

Coping with the Shock of Accidental Death

"I'd left the back door open so Dixie could run in and out. . . . I repeatedly checked on her. But one time I went to the window and didn't see her. My blood ran cold. I raced outside to one side of the house. No Dixie. Went to the other side. No Dixie. I ran back through the house and out the front door; I looked to my left, and there she was, across the street on one corner. So I called her. She started to come back. . . . Out of the corner of my eye, I saw a van fly by and run over her."

When an emergency case arrives at any large urban animal hospital like the VHUP, there's an automatic rush of activity. Veterinarians and nurses move with calm, brisk authority. At the same time you may be going through an intensely emotional reaction, one as strong as if you'd had a brush with death yourself. Strange as they seem, both reactions to awful accidents are accepted as the norm in the emergency service; no one will think you're out of place for crying at a time like that, and the clinicians' quick action is necessary for your pet's sake. It's also likely that you won't notice much of the commotion. Your mind is more likely to stray back to the scene of the accident you discovered or witnessed, replaying what happened. The pain you felt when you first saw your animal's injured body is so strong you'll recall it for many months to come.

My own glimpses of what happens in accidental pet deaths on the street and in the home come from owners like Rae, a thirty-three-year-old Mississippi woman. She was so tormented by memories of her dog's death that she described it in a lengthy letter, letting me see what it was like to "watch in frozen horror as a van ran over Dixie," her tiny Chihuahua.

"I live on one corner of a four-way intersection," she wrote. "I'd left the back door open so Dixie could run in and out. She was out back where I could see her from the house, and I repeatedly checked on her. But one time I went to the window and didn't see her. My blood ran cold. I raced outside to one side of the house. No Dixie. Went to the other side. No Dixie. I ran back through the house and out the front door; I looked to my left, and there she was, across the street on one corner. So I called to her. She started to come back. I can't remember whether she stopped to smell something in the street, but out of the corner of my eye I saw a van fly by and run over her.

"The horror of it was that the back part of her body was lying on the street, and she was up on her front legs," Rae continued. "She just arched her head back, and then went down. My God, it was just like hell on earth for me. I ran over to her. Her insides were partially out, and I saw her front legs twitch. So help me, I thought she was still alive—but I never believed she'd survive that awful injury.

"The guy who hit her came back and apologized, but I was crying so hard I never looked at him, just got his name. Now I can't figure how he *couldn't* have seen her; she was in the middle of the street. I feel now I could kill this guy; I wouldn't do it, but that's how I feel."

Despite her anger at the driver, Rae wrote even more extensively about her *own* responsibility for Dixie's death—a guilt so strong it seemed to outweigh every other feeling. "You will never find anyone who loves dogs like I do," she wrote. "I've never had a pet that met with a tragic death before, especially not a death that was my fault. How should I deal with this hell I'm going through? Dixie made me so happy, and I had a hand in her death. How can I have peace of mind knowing I was the cause of her death? I should have been watching her. I loved her like she was my child; she was my only source of happiness, and I enjoyed every moment with her. The thought of getting another dog is no help—it's Dixie I want back. Another dog wouldn't make me stop thinking of what I let happen to her. The pain I feel is absolute heartbreak. It's always *if* I hadn't let her out, or *if* I had watched her. I'd give the world to have her back."

Rae was troubled by the movements she saw Dixie make in her last moments. The motion made as little sense as the accident. She wrote, "I just can't forget the horror I saw with my own eyes. Please advise me. Did she *not* die a fast death? Why did she rise on her front legs like that? If she died immediately, would she have tried to get up that way? Please help me—I just see her over and over, trying to get up after she'd been hit." The pain she thought she'd detected in Dixie's movements made Rae feel even worse because it eliminated one of her few possible comforts: the chance her dog's death had been quick and painless.

After consulting several veterinarians on our staff I was able to reassure Rae that Dixie had probably died instantly—and that what she had seen were post-death movements, occurring after the dog lost all feeling. I knew that would be hard to accept, even with professional assurance. Like most people, Rae associated movement of any kind with life rather than death. And that motion made it easier in some ways for her to focus on Dixie's nightmarish accident, turning it over in her mind as she struggled with her loss. That concentration was actually fortunate; it meant Rae had begun to work through the initial adjustment of bereavement rather than deny the death—a sure sign she would someday accept and resolve her loss. The guilt and anger she felt reflected Dixie's importance in her life and were natural responses to the end of a precious relationship.

As encouraging as those factors seemed to me, I knew Rae would find scant comfort from any aspect of her deprivation at first. She wanted her dog back—and with that dog, the chance to prepare for Dixie's peaceful demise rather than the swift and violent accident that killed her. But accidental deaths leave no opportunity for saddened owners to control the situation. If your pet dies naturally you can usually accept that his "time had come," whether you attribute it to old age, disease, or simply the will of God. When you choose euthanasia for him you can do so only if you consider it the best alternative for him. Often in those cases you have some time to prepare for the death, even if only a few hours. You might be able to control the manner or place of your pet's death, insisting it happen at home, arranging for the hospital care, or scheduling a euthanasia injection when it seems appropriate. Such control may give you the chance to say good-bye to your pet and to comfort yourself that his death is peaceful. Rae had none of those assurances. There's no logical reason, no acceptable cause for a pet's accidental death—even blaming it on God's will makes that will seem unnecessarily cruel. No owner in Rae's place could see this death-by-chance as the best alternative; few people dream this alternative exists for their well-tended pets. Worst of all, accidental deaths usually happen so quickly and unexpectedly the owners have no time to prepare, to say good-bye, or to arrange a peaceful last moment. Memories of violence and your visceral reactions will add shock, fear, horror, and intensified guilt to the more common reactions other owners face.

When you seek my help after your animal dies in an accident, my greatest challenge is to help you understand the incomprehensible, to grasp and accept the bizarre situation that began in or near the home and ended in the hospital emergency room, usually within a few hours. You'll probably begin this understanding by searching your mind for any reason or hint related to the death—but no matter how many times you replay the accident in your mind, no real reasons can be found. None exist. These deaths are called senseless or random because *no logic stands behind them*. It's part of my task to help you accept that an accident, by definition, can't be an event that *you* caused knowingly or purposefully. You may think you were in control, and therefore a cause, but in reality no one could have stopped the accident. So I work with you to prove your guilt is normal but unjustified; to cope with the strong emotions that match the horrible death you now mourn; to understand more clearly how risk affects your pet's life and your ownership, and to reestablish the control taken from you when your animal died by chance.

"I Can't Sleep, Knowing What I Did!"

It's easiest to understand the sense of self-blame and responsibility in the owners whose actions really *did* lead to their pets' accidental deaths; such feelings may be strongest in those persons. Hazel, a woman in her fifties, wrote to tell me about an accidental death that may be more common than she suspected: she ran over one of her Pekingese puppies in her own driveway, killing it instantly. "Believe me, I know what hell is," she wrote. "There have been many nights since when I can't sleep, knowing what I did. It was a freak accident, and I have to learn to live with it—but I still can't accept it." Ruth, another woman who killed her fifteen-year-old cat, Barnaby, in the same way, reviewed what happened to find evidence of her guilt. "I broke my routine," she said. "Usually, I eat lunch at the office, so Barnaby gets let out—and back in—once before I leave for work in the morning. That day I stopped home at lunch to drop off some bakery goods I'd bought and let him out. He stayed out all afternoon, as he does sometimes on weekends. When I came home he ran up the driveway just ahead of the car to greet me, but I didn't see him—he must have looked away from the car or he'd have seen it coming. Worst of all, I didn't even know for a few moments I'd run over him. There was no thump. I parked, and then I heard him yowling with pain. It's a sound I'll never forget."

Neither Hazel nor Ruth anticipated they might kill their own pets, but now they can't see their actions as blameless and unintentional. They're just two of the many owners who don't consider the words "It was an accident" to be an excuse, as they would if the results were just close calls. Humans have accepted the concept of no-fault insurance, named for those times when no one can determine who's to blame when cars crash but no one is killed. But few can apply that same concept to fatal accidents, particularly when the victim is a helpless pet for whom you feel responsible. Even owners who were miles away when their pets died accidently blame themselves. The natural response is to see your caring as deficient, to switch your self-image from dedicated owner to delinquent. It doesn't matter whether your dog runs into traffic, your bird flies into a clear windowpane, or your kitten ingests a stray needle caught in the carpet. You're haunted by "if onlys" and "should haves"—whether you see yourself as directly involved or just negligent. That's why Rae, who saw someone else kill her dog, can believe she "had a hand" in Dixie's death. Even though she described her frequent checks through the window, Rae later accused herself with the words, "I should have watched her."

If that's how you feel when your pet dies by chance, you face an insurmountable challenge: "How can I find peace of mind knowing I was the cause of her death?" as Rae put it. You can't. As long as you blame yourself for a situation that was out of anyone's control, you will not be able to resolve your guilt and grief. Think about the responsibility you're claiming: in accusing yourself of killing your pet are you demanding an impossible level of power over the situation that hurt you? Ruth and Hazel, for instance, would have had to see straight through their cars—as well as control their animals' vision—in order to prevent those deaths. Rae would have had to see Dixie not only when she looked through a window, but when she turned her back to the view. Once Dixie had made her way to the street Rae even wished she could have controlled the driver's vision. Like most pet owners, all three women assumed they'd always be able to protect their pets. The fatal accidents make it clear they never completely had that power—a realization not one of them yet wants to acknowledge.

That's why you may need another person's perspective when your pet dies in an accident. The event shatters not only your relationship but destroys your most basic beliefs about your role as a responsible, caring pet owner. It's also likely your usual clear thinking will be confused by your shock and horror; guilt and anger can cloud the facts and details as well. An objective listener can point out that the words "I'd give anything to have him back" indicate your blamelessness as much as anything else. If that attitude is heartfelt, as I know it must be, how could anyone, even you, accuse you of willfully and knowingly killing your pet? Someone may be able to show you why you feel so uncomfortably guilty and angry at this time: because the accident reminds you that your pet faces risks every day, dangers you can't prevent. It's unpleasant to consider those risks, and far easier to assume the responsibility, as painful as your guilt may be. But blaming yourself won't reverse the accident, make your grief any easier, or give you the control you really didn't have at the time. If you can come to see the accident as an *accident*—a death by chance rather than by your hand—you'll be better able to cope with your loss.

"We Took the Wrong Chance": Accepting Risk

Jack and Nina Krasker were a childless couple in their thirties who solved the problems of keeping an apartment pet in a popular way: their rabbit, Farley, didn't make excessive noise or scratch furniture. He was as cuddly as a kitten and as playful as a pup but required neither indoor barriers nor outdoor exercise. Nina even taught him to use a litterbox. "He was, without doubt, a hassle-free pet," she said. Even when they noticed some unusual lumps beneath his skin, the problem turned out to be a fatty mass, not threatening to his health. "We were relieved to know nothing was wrong—the doctors were quite sure Farley would be okay for a long time," Jack recalled.

Still, when the VHUP veterinarian discussed the fatty mass with the couple, they asked whether it could be removed surgically; now that they noticed it, they hoped an operation could be done for purely cosmetic reasons. They listened carefully while the veterinarian explained the many risks of surgery on a rabbit; like many exotic types of pets, rabbits are difficult to anesthetize. He told them Farley stood a less than normal chance of surviving this surgery, cosmetic or not. But the Kraskers had confidence in Farley and in the surgeons and anesthesiologists; they approved the operation despite the risk. So when their rabbit died in the operating room the next day, they were shocked and heartbroken. "We took the wrong chance," said Jack when he and Nina came to my office. "The worst that could happen happened. It makes sense. We knew it might happen, but we didn't really accept it as a reality, you know?"

Even though Jack and Nina knew the blame really lay with the odds, they felt awful because they knew those odds in advance and still authorized the operation. The grim reality of the risk factor weighted their guilt. Because the surgery wasn't really necessary, Farley's death seemed even more pointless.

That struggle to see remote possibilities as real threats goes on every day when a pet dies accidentally. Until that awful moment when you realize, as Jack said, "the worst that could happen has happened," you probably dismiss the thought of danger. Many owners find it impossible to imagine their faithful and well-loved dogs would dash in front of traffic or that their cats might be enticed by an open window with a hundred-foot fall just beyond the sill. Those who own exotic animals are particularly susceptible to misunderstanding the severity of risks for their pets. Snake owners, for instance, often fail to realize their pets can sustain sprains or breaks when they fall from high perches to the floor; the snake's long, supple shape doesn't necessarily mean he can't hurt himself. Rabbits, birds, and other exotics are usually difficult to treat with assurance; they may have unusually fragile physical features, their reactions to medication may be unusual or unknown, and veterinarians may not have enough experience to correct their problems. In many cases the risks for exotic pets are even higher because these animals were never meant to live outside the wild. Although dogs and cats have been domesticated for centuries, many other types of pets haven't yet adapted to our life-styles. But even people who own the more common cats and dogs find themselves shocked by risks they never imagined. The myths that cats have nine lives, can survive falls without injury, or have natural and peerless balance are just some examples of why so many owners ignore apparent dangers. But cats *do* clamber out of windows and fall from tall buildings; dogs *do* stray in front of cars or stop to smell something on a busy street. Wild and domesticated birds do mistake glass for open flying space, and all types of pet animals die in surgery, in poisonings from household chemicals, or in some accidental self-injury.

It's easier for someone like me to see those risks as things to expect; I encounter the evidence outside my office at all hours of every day. But few owners have extensive experience with accidents and certainly try to avoid those risks they can anticipate. That lack of experience sometimes makes the real danger seem vague and distant. If it hasn't happened yet, they think, why expect it? What's more, if you feel you've done everything possible for your animal, it's difficult to acknowledge that some unpredictable risk could undo all your hard work and loving attention. To do so would be to say you haven't done enough for your pet—no matter how impossible total protection might be. Of course ignorance or failure to recognize dangers to your pet are just unfortunate realities, not real failures. You shouldn't carry your worries about a pet's safety to extremes, so that your concern prevents you from leaving your home or finding time to focus on other interests. One of the pleasures in your relationships with pets comes from that chance to relax, to feel secure and safe. I do recommend you learn about those risks that are considered most common: car accidents, falls, substance poisonings in and around the home, swallowable objects in the home, and other dangers. Your veterinarian can tell you how to prepare for and handle emergency situations to some extent. Once you've made those efforts you'll better understand the potential for risk in your pet's life—and perhaps ensure that his life will be a little safer.

"What Would You Say to Me?": Senseless Pain

It's difficult to say unequivocally that certain types of deaths are more senseless or devastating than others, but it's natural for owners whose pets die accidentally to see their heartache as the ultimate grief. That's particularly true if the accident was extremely violent, totally unpredictable, and painful. Megan was an owner who wrote me several months after her poodle died to explain that lonely viewpoint:

"I recently read an article about how you help people through their grief when they lose their pets. I also noticed that most of the pets mentioned died of natural causes or had to be put to sleep. My little poodle, Shannon, just four pounds, was attacked by a German shepherd several months ago. He ripped open her stomach and her insides were falling out. I can't forget how she looked at me as if to say, 'Why me? Help me!' I rushed her to the emergency service, where she died in surgery thirty minutes later. I was devastated. I felt like I was burying a baby, and I can't forget how she died. She didn't deserve to die in such a cruel manner. And when I read the article, I kept thinking, 'What would Jamie say to me?' If you could find time, I would really appreciate an answer. I still cry every day. I visit her grave at least twice a week. I try to remember all the happiness she brought into my life, but the more I remember the more I cry. I just want her back. I can't help my feelings—I try not to cry, but she was such a big part of my life!"

Megan's lingering distress was no different from the pain I see in owners after any type of accidental death. Long after the sense of guilt eases, the recollection of those last tortured moments prompts haunted feelings, depression, and despair. Megan's recovery was slower and more agonizing because she could graphically recall her poodle's violent death. Her repeated attempts to stop crying and to substitute happy memories for her mourning failed because she had to express her sorrow more than she'd expected. She seemed almost more worried about her tears than about the improbability of Shannon's violent death.

That's why I told Megan not to hold back any of her emotions or tears. Shannon's awful end *naturally* spurred awful feelings. Her reactions were not excessive but appropriate; crying every day and visiting the grave frequently were logical ways of coping with a senseless tragedy. Her mourning for Shannon was complex: she had lost her companion, the chance to see her pet die naturally and comfortably, her control over Shannon's safety, and everything she cherished in their relationship. And because the manner of loss was severe, more swift and violent than usual, I'd expect her sorrow to be equally severe. Had she lived close enough to Philadelphia to see me in person, I might simply have sat with her as she cried, holding her hand and waiting for her to talk when she felt able to express herself.

Sometimes that's all you can do for someone who's experienced such a horrible accident and the death that followed. Megan seemed to know her best comfort came from visiting Shannon's grave and in ventilating her emotions. Those efforts helped her slowly to accept that death, once only a vague threat, had been real. I pointed out that she'd already made progress by focusing on her loss rather than dwelling on the manner of her dog's death. Just by writing to ask for help Megan showed she had regained some control. And that's what I told her, as I have so many other owners in similar situations.

"I'm Afraid It Might Happen Again"

When Joan, a twenty-three-year-old single woman, brought home her puppy, Bloomer, she took care to make his new home as safe as possible. She taught him to stay in the kitchen, with the help of barriers, when she left the house. She gave him a firm "No!" when he tried to tangle with dangerous objects. Her household cleaners were stored on high cabinet shelves, and she never took him outside without his leash firmly attached. But despite her precautions she came home one day to find Bloomer dead in her kitchen.

"It was my first day back at work after vacation," she recalled when she wrote me. "We'd just spent a great week together, taking long walks and playing every day. But when I returned home that night I could see what had happened. Bloomer died when he tangled his neck up in the handles of a tote bag and choked to death." Obviously, Joan never imagined the cloth tote posed a threat to Bloomer's safety and left it within reach.

Now, three months after her puppy's death, Joan said she'd been able to "ease the guilt, although I still feel the loss. I still cry when I think about him. But I miss having a puppy in the house, and would like to have another. It's so hard to decide, not just because I miss Bloomer, but because I'm afraid something like this could happen again."

Although it's often difficult for people to consider another pet, the decision takes on grim significance when an animal under your care dies accidentally. No matter how calm and controlled life seemed with your previous pet, his fatal accident may haunt you. It's natural to worry that another accidental death might follow the first if you bring home a new pet. Joan probably would never leave a tote bag lying around her kitchen again, but she will forever wonder whether she'll miss some equally dangerous but innocuous-looking risk.

Such worries are a normal hurdle in your bereavement for a pet who dies by chance. You'll probably feel somewhat skittish for a while, perhaps almost overcautious if you're unwilling to take even the slightest risks. You'll at least take more care than ever with your new pet or your remaining ones, perhaps leashing dogs even if you never liked to restrain them before or confining cats to your home instead of allowing them to meander. Those aren't problematic responses, just practical ones, considering the death your pet experienced. Again, remind yourself *no amount of preparation can guarantee complete safety*. You might well miss another risk in or around your home, as Joan feared she would. But if you have considered and corrected as many dangerous items and areas as possible, you should feel relatively secure about bringing another animal into your home. If you feel ready to do that you've accepted your blamelessness for your pet's death and your new responsibility for the next animal.

5

Handling Special Bereavement Problems

"I don't know what to tell my child because I don't know what to tell myself. I can't search for him forever; there's been no trace of him in the area. But what happened? Is he dead, or stolen, or just wandering? What if he comes back someday? We've thought about getting another dog, but I'm not sure I'm ready for that; I keep worrying Finnegan might return."

Stella wasn't really Jumper's owner, and the cat wasn't dead. Still she wrote to me, so troubled she ended her letter in a way no other owner has: "I don't really feel better for having told you about this. I think I feel worse." Yet, like almost any typical owner, her awful feelings followed the end of a loving relationship with a pet, in this case "the little cat from next door that was abandoned by his student owner who moved and left him behind."

Here's how Stella described her chance meeting with Jumper: "He appeared in the middle of July. He followed my cat into the kitchen and helped himself to her food. My cat didn't like him, of course. That was the problem. I couldn't keep him because he made my cat's life miserable. He wanted to live with us. He wanted to be my cat. But I couldn't even let him in at night because of my own cat. Once he was out all night in a rainstorm, and I couldn't sleep even though I knew the back porch was fairly dry for him. I ran out at 3 A.M. and wrapped him in a towel, holding him in my arms. Even though he really doesn't like to be held, he purred so sweetly."

Jumper endeared himself to Stella partly because "he had a horrible background. He'd been owned by a gang of male college students who enjoyed slapping the floor to make him jump; that's why they called him Jumper," she wrote. "The person who came looking for him was sitting for him for the summer. She was gone most of every week, and her male roommates would close Jumper's access window to the house. He seemed to fear males, but he seemed to love me so much that I decided to take care of him. He didn't really know how to jump into my lap, but he'd lie on his side with his little head nestled against my leg, purring contentedly. He was long and thin, with long legs, and a beautiful peach-colored belly and feet. His tail was always held high. He tried very hard to ingratiate himself with our whole family, but he never succeeded with my cat." So Stella began to look for another home for him. She put notices on bulletin boards, called friends, and even contacted the local animal shelter once, although her heart wasn't in it. "It was horrible," she wrote. "Two men from the humane society and I were chasing him, trying to catch him. We couldn't. I cried for hours. I was glad he had escaped."

Finally, Stella thought of a better solution—taking Jumper to the nearby state university, where he could live and work as a mouser in one of the animal barns. "The son of one of my friends works at the sheep barn, and he came to get Jumper," she recalled. "He caught him and put him into a box; Jumper was wild with terror, struggling and screaming and biting Bill's hand savagely in the process." Despite his resistance, Jumper did stay in his new home at the university barn, and Stella began to mourn the loss of her transient friend. "Now I feel so guilty," she wrote. "I betrayed a loving friend. It's so hard to see through my tears. I didn't think I could keep him, but I miss him so much I'm almost virtually unable to function."

Even though Stella had thought about her feelings of devotion for the stray cat, and had resolved his homelessness, she seemed puzzled by her reactions. Her guilt and depression were almost as strong as if Jumper had died, mimicking the feelings she'd have had after choosing euthanasia because her final choice controlled Jumper's fate. I could see that even his death might have been easier for her to accept; then she might comfort herself that he was at peace. But because she saw him leave struggling, and knew he was alive, she imagined him lonely, frightened, and rejected yet again. Her grief had no logical end in sight, none of the finality of death-related bereavement, but all the same reactions. A little part of Stella seemed to have been carted away with Jumper when he left.

I was able to tell Stella her guilty and depressed reactions to this special kind of loss were completely normal. She had to know she'd done the right thing in order to accept Jumper's new life and her role in choosing it for him. I knew from my own experience that farm animals are both valued by their caretakers and usually happy in their environment and told her so. What's more, I reviewed with her all the decisions she made for Jumper. Her temporary adoption, caring acts, and search for a new home for the stray all demonstrated she hadn't betrayed him. Another person might have refused the cat entry to her home or simply called the authorities to remove him from her property. Stella had found the right balance in caring for Jumper as well as considering her own cat's needs; it was easy to reassure her she'd acted with the animals' best interests in mind.

Stella's bereavement was as real as the grief you feel when a pet dies, and possibly more confusing. Her emotions were similar to those I've seen in other people whose loss of ownership is distressing, causing grief and mourning whether the pet dies or remains alive. The loss of ownership can be as great as the loss of a pet's life. For Stella that role as Jumper's owner was fleeting but strong. For people whose pets run away, ownership loss can be either temporary or permanent; even if the animal eventually returns, the owner's grief can be severe. Some owners can't control their animals' violent or dangerous behavior, and must choose to end the relationship however much they love the pet, faults and all. In most of these special cases the owners find themselves unable to control the relationship in a satisfying way, and those frustrating circumstances create an intense sorrow. One of my own experiences with grief falls into this category, so I feel a special commitment to these owners. I know what it feels like to give up two happy, healthy dogs, losing the chance to see what happened to them. The simultaneous, forced losses of Duchess and Taffy were no easier because they didn't involve death—in some ways they were *more* intense. So when you grieve for a stray, a runaway, a vicious biter, or a pet who can't move with you, you can expect potent and puzzling feelings. The best way to handle these special problems is to take or regain as much control as you can so that, like Stella, you can look back and say "I did my best as an owner for the pet I lost."

"He Could Be Dead, and I Wouldn't Know"

When your pet runs away you're left with an ambiguous ownership role: the animal is gone but you're still responsible for him. So you grieve your loss even as you conduct a frantic search and remain hopeful but feel extremely helpless. You're sure every passing moment increases the awful risks for your pet but you can't imagine what those risks might be—nothing will be certain until or unless you find him, dead or alive. It's a situation that guarantees rising panic and sinking hopes, emotions that complicate your search even more. "I started by driving around the neighborhood, trying to spot Pickles," recalled Nan. "But after the first afternoon I had to continue on foot. I kept imagining I'd see her dead in the street, around the next corner as I drove." That panic remained with Nan even after the local animal shelter called to let her know someone had found her dog. "The guy saw her walking the yellow line on the busiest street in town, nearly getting hit every few seconds," she recalled. "He let her jump into his car, and called the shelter when he got home. When he told me that I shuddered—I was scared until the moment I saw her alive, playing in his yard."

Lillian, another owner who made a systematic search for her cat, Mack, remembered "crying nonstop while I put posters up all over the neighborhood. I knew then how I'd feel if Mack died. Over and over I thought, 'He could be dead now, and I wouldn't know.' But I kept looking; to give up would be like saying 'He *is* dead,' and I couldn't face that possibility."

Most owners of lost pets find their first grief-stricken reaction is denial; it's almost necessary in this situation. Your fear of the unknown can intensify denial when your pet runs away, causing you to hear your cat or dog scratching at your door when the noise really comes from somewhere else. And if your search continues unsuccessfully for a long time, denial can grow even stronger, prompting you to view your pet's escape unrealistically. One owner remained convinced his dog was alive many months after the active search stopped. Because he lived near a university-based veterinary hospital, he was sure someone had taken his dog and sold her as a research animal—even though the hospital officials told him that violated their policy. Gruesome as it sounds, the thought that his dog was taken by force was easier for him to handle than the chance she might have died lost and alone in the woods around his house. His reasoning also helped him combat the very natural guilt he felt for "shirking" his responsibility. But it didn't really resolve his grief at all; the dangerous delusion he nurtured only added insult to injury and kept him from facing uncomfortable facts.

Fortunately, excessively strong denial isn't common to the owners of runaway pets. Guilt is far more prevalent, causing you to blame yourself for the loss and swear it'll never happen again—if you can only find your pet alive. Like the owners whose pets die in accidents, twenty-twenty hindsight shows you the open window or door, the unclipped leash or unlatched cage, or the moment you turned your back—signs of owner failure. The one benefit you have here is the chance to set that mistake right, to find your pet. That's why most people find it impossible simply to sit and wait for a pet's return, and why they rarely experience initial depression, anger, or denial. Neighborhood searches, lost-pet notices, and calls to friends and area shelters increase the chance of finding your pet and lessen the impact of your feelings.

Of course you won't be able to conduct your search twenty-four hours a day. You may find your strong emotions most troubling in those hours when you can't be out looking for your runaway animal, and it's important for you to think about what you're feeling during those down times. Remember you are really no more to blame than any owner whose pet dies; your distress indicates just how strongly you *do* care for your animal, not your deficiency as an owner. Try to notice whether denial is in anyway thwarting your search. If you can't bring yourself to admit your pet might have headed into the next county, or toward a major highway near your house, your attempts to find him might not succeed. Some owners avoid calling their local animal control and animal shelter services because they're unwilling to admit their pets might be given away or killed by euthanasia in those places if they're unclaimed. *That's* a form of denial that can only hurt you. I recommend reporting your runaway immediately to those agencies, since their efforts automatically supply them with information about countless lost and found pets. And you should be ready to ask for help at this time. One of the great surprises of your search can be others' willingness to assist you and your pet.

Because your pet's absence alters your routines and your relationship just as his death would, you should also think and talk about why you miss him so much, why the house seems so empty without him. The insights you gain will remind you you've been a caring, responsible owner—that you still *are* such an owner. What's more, you can use those thoughts to understand your actions, giving yourself hope as well as convincing others your pet is still important to you. If you can prove to yourself and to others that this search is vital to your happiness, you'll feel far more comfortable asking for help or taking time off from work to look for your animal.

Your reactions to the loss of a runaway pet change, however, when you begin to suspect he might never return. The emotions that fueled your active search may seem to start all over again but more intensely—and you can easily imagine your pain will never end because you mourn for a potentially unresolvable loss. For Leila, a Dallas woman, her mourning involved anger and guilt, by turns. She wasn't sure whether her purebred collie, Finnegan, had been stolen or had simply escaped from his yard enclosure; when he'd been gone for a few weeks, and her search seemed futile, she called me to ask what she should do. The problem, she told me, was with her six-year-old daughter. They lived in a neighborhood filled almost exclusively by childless families, and her daughter's primary playmate after school had been Finnegan. I suspected the dog meant as much to Leila as to her child. Her husband's job kept him traveling most of the time, and she mentioned many examples of the time she spent grooming and exercising this special pet. Her daughter had begun to cry at night and was listless during the after-school hours she used to spend with the dog. Leila finally admitted she got angry whenever she thought of someone stealing Finnegan, then switched to anxious guilt because she felt responsible for his mysterious escape. "I don't know what to tell my child because I don't know what to tell myself," she said. "I can't search for him forever; there's been no trace of him in the area. But what happened? Is he dead, or stolen, or just wandering? What if he comes back someday? We've thought about getting another dog, but I'm not sure I'm ready for that. I keep worrying that Finnegan might return."

There were no sure answers to any of Leila's questions, as natural as they were. I did tell her, however, that she would have to be honest with her daughter and with herself. At this point it seemed logical to assume Finnegan would not come back. I also told her it was far more likely he had escaped on his own and that she could therefore assume he probably hadn't been stolen. Wandering from his yard enclosure left three possibilities, none of them hopeful: Finnegan could be dead naturally, killed in an accident, or adopted by someone who'd found him straying. The first two seemed most likely to Leila because she'd notified so many animal shelters in her area, giving them Finnegan's distinctive coloring and the numbers on his tags. She felt that anyone who might have found him alive would have called her phone number, which was also listed on his tags.

Ultimately, we agreed that Leila would try to accept the most dreadful, yet helpful, possibility: Finnegan had died. That choice was both painful and practical because it allowed her to focus on something definite rather than continue struggling with an unresolved, unfinished loss. Of course resolving his death was still difficult because she couldn't see any proof of it. She lacked the chance to cremate or bury him, or even the opportunity to consider those options. But I told her she and her family should feel comfortable going through the rest of the mourning process, perhaps holding a memorial service or simply talking about how special Finnegan's companionship had been in their lives. We talked twice more in the weeks that followed, and although Leila put off her decision to get another dog, she found some relief for her confusing feelings in the acceptance of her dog's death. If you face a similar situation you may have to accept the awful thought of your pet's death simply so you can resolve your emotions and move forward with your life. It may help you to seek professional advice, to hear your veterinarian explain that death is a distinct possibility, and to gain some confirmation for your need to resolve this loss. Because you went through some bereavement reactions when your animal first ran away, you may be prepared for the more intense feelings you'll have now.

"I Don't Want to Give Huey Up"

Marian Jackson called me in tears; for the first few moments after I answered the phone, she couldn't speak. So I just encouraged her to cry and waited until she felt calm enough to explain her problem. She'd called about Huey, her two-year-old black Labrador retriever. She and her husband bought the dog at the request of their young son, who was terminally ill. But after Huey had been in their home for four months, the boy died. Since then the couple's daughter had grown up and moved into her own home, and Huey had become even more precious to the Jacksons. The problem began when Marian and her husband decided to sell their large house and move to a condominium complex. "We're both uncomfortable with all that space for just the two of us," she told me, "and this condo is exactly what we want in a new home. But just as we were about to close, I realized that Huey wouldn't be able to live outdoors as he has all along. And there's so little space indoors. George put off the closing because I was so upset, but we have to decide soon or we'll lose the chance to buy. And I don't want to give Huey up."

I asked Marian to tell me more about Huey and why he was so special to her. "Normally, I don't like pets very much," she said, "but I just had to fall in love with Huey. He just loved the entire family, especially my son. He seemed to grieve with us, and to comfort us. And he's never been a trouble; I don't know what I'd have done without him. That makes it even harder to just give him up now for a new home. What should I do?"

Marian seemed convinced the condominium was indeed the Jacksons' best choice for a home and felt it "wouldn't be fair" to keep the dog confined indoors; at the same time she didn't want herself or her husband to resent the dog for preventing the move. She was close to accepting a forced separation from Huey but held back her decision because she had no idea how to find him a good home. Euthanasia wasn't an option—"that would be cruel, although some people have suggested it. You'll never see a dog in such good shape," she told me. Indeed, because Huey was a purebred and had been so carefully tended, I pointed out that he had excellent chances for adoption. At my suggestion she began to contact veterinarians, Lab breeders, and friends who had enough room for a large dog. I also suggested Marian consider finding a home for Huey that would allow her to visit him periodically—perhaps a friend, a local breeder, or a farm owner could keep him and help ease the separation with visiting privileges. She liked that last possibility best; it was the thought of never seeing Huey again that bothered Marian most. The last time we talked she was feeling reassured by the offers she'd solicited and was considering which would provide "the best of homes" for Huey.

When Marian realized she could, to some extent, control what seemed to be a forced separation from her dog, she began to feel better. But she was fortunate. Even if her search had failed she could have kept Huey in the new condo until another home was available. Many owners don't have that option. They may not be able to afford the apartments and homes that allow pets and have to move from their current residences for a variety of reasons. Although the priority of the family's shelter comes first, their dedication to their animals is strong and makes the move to a new life even more difficult. Sometimes they feel forced into giving up the pet even when no housing rules prohibit animals; that's often the case with people whose jobs change to include more frequent overtime hours and business trips, opportunities for advancement that prevent consistent ownership. In any of these situations you face a dilemma fraught with pain. You may feel guilty for choosing something less personal—a house, a job, a move—over your pet, as if somehow that choice proves you don't love your animal.

Of course that's not true. If you really didn't care about your pet you wouldn't spend time agonizing over the problem. In most cases you can justify your choice by thinking of what's best for the animal and what's best for you. If your job will keep you away from home for many hours or days at a time, you won't be able to give your pet regular exercise, food, and attention; your absence might well prompt him to misbehave out of boredom, potentially allowing for the destruction of your home and belongings. Your move to a "no pets" apartment or building will not be easy if you try to hide an

animal's presence and could result in eviction if you dis-
obey that rule. And a move to a smaller home can be
frustrating for both owner and pet if they had always
had plenty of space before. You'll have to do more to
ensure that he gets enough exercise, and he may not
adjust well to the changed environment of your new
home.

Once you've weighed those and other factors, and
have reached a decision, you may face the additional
problem of finding someone to adopt your pet. If your
search is unsuccessful your guilt and anxiety are apt to
intensify, as Aileen's did. When she was ordered by her
doctor to stop living by herself and enter a nursing
home, she had no alternative but euthanasia for her pets.
The sixty-seven-year-old woman was living with an
eighteen-year-old poodle whose heart and eyes were
failing, as well as two cats, aged twelve and two. "It
was easier to have Peaches, my poodle, put down," she
wrote from her New Jersey nursing home, "because I
knew he didn't have much longer to live. But the cats
were healthy and relatively young. I was with them
every step of the way, but I did not feel proud of myself.
They would never have done such a thing to me." Aileen knew her medical problems might cause her own
death sometime in the near future and almost resented
her chance to stay alive with full-time care because that
chance included no options for her pets. As a result she
entered her new life with a deep sense of guilt and
anger—feelings that were still strong when she wrote to
me two years after entering the nursing home. "This
terrible guilt just will not leave me no matter how I try
to overcome it," she wrote. "There are few who understand. I'm supposed to put it out of my mind and go on
to something else. But there is little else to go on to
when you reach almost seventy and are in the position

that many old people are forced into. We need legislation that will allow people in rest homes to keep their longtime pets—they would probably act far better than medicine."

Aileen had reached a conclusion we've been studying at the Penn Center for the Interaction of Animals and Society: the desire and apparent need to allow pet ownership in long-term-care facilities such as hers. I was able to tell her something about that research and, more important, to remind her that loss of ownership was "the system's fault," not hers. Today many nursing homes *do* allow at least a community pet, but there's little to help someone facing Aileen's predicament. Had she received counseling to help her make the adjustment to the nursing home, she might have learned about other options for her pets, or at least received more support for her triple euthanasia decision. Feeling forced into a separation from your animals is distressing enough, but to feel pressured into choosing their deaths must be even more heartbreaking. That's why I encouraged Aileen to keep "talking" to me through letters, to relieve the helpless and unexpressed feelings she'd held in for two years, and since she couldn't come to the hospital to see me in person. I wanted her to have the support that was apparently lacking in her new home; rather than tell her to "go on to something else," I agreed that she had to think her way through this unfair and bewildering dilemma. As we corresponded I think she was able to see some justification to ease her guilt. The euthanasia choice was certainly appropriate for Peaches, the elderly poodle. For her cats she could at least rely on the assurance they'd had a peaceful, painless death, which she considered better than relinquishing them to an animal shelter.

You're likely to have more options than Aileen did when you must find a new home for your pet. Don't dismiss the effectiveness of advertisements, animal-shelter adoption services, or even word-of-mouth contacts through friends and relatives. Most of the pet owners I've counseled in this situation do everything possible to find housing alternatives for their pets; that's necessary in order to combat the guilt inherent in giving up a beloved animal. If, after you examine all the options, euthanasia seems the only viable choice, you should recognize and resolve your feelings before you authorize that humane death. As you adjust to this decision keep reminding yourself of how much you've cared for your pet in the past. The pain you feel now reflects that dedication and ensures you'll never forget the years you spent as that animal's loving owner. It's as important to pay attention to *your* feelings as to his future options.

"In Spite of It All, We Miss Him Terribly"

When your pet has a serious behavior problem—one that makes it impossible to keep him in your home, such as destructive behavior or biting—you have even fewer options than the owners who can't move their pets to a new home. These are, in most cases, the pets that can't be given away; if they pose a serious danger to your family the problem isn't likely to disappear in someone else's home. Still, you're apt to make every effort to keep your pet and will probably choose euthanasia for him only with great difficulty. Despite the damage the animal can do, you can still love him.

In this unusual situation you should realize that most animal behavior problems are changeable through behavior modification, medication, environmental changes, or some combination of treatments. Most do not merit euthanasia. If your animal is self-destructive, a property destroyer, or a threat to your family's safety, you should first consult a qualified behaviorist or veterinarian. A professional can observe your pet's behavior, learn about your interactions with the animal, and then assess the situation. With that advice you can choose from several options. If all attempts to correct his behavior fail, you and your veterinarian can discuss euthanasia as a last resort.

Nelson and Barbara Chambers, like many owners with problem pets, had been considering euthanasia for Charger, their biting springer spaniel. But first they worked with the Penn Animal Behavior Clinic at our hospital to correct Charger's problem. Our clinic staff helped them to change the dog's environment, to retrain him, and to cope with their ambivalence about his violent behavior. The couple worked so hard at these changes that they were frequent visitors to the VHUP. Despite those efforts, Charger's attacks grew more unpredictable and violent. I visited them at their Philadelphia home one weekend to see the dog and to talk about euthanasia. One week later they chose that last resort, and they wrote to tell me about their reactions to his death:

"You were hardly the villain," Barbara wrote at the start of her letter. "We'd essentially decided in December that this was inevitable, but put it off to give him one last shot by working with the trainer. Talking with you really helped us to review his behavior in chronological order. It was as if Charger were a textbook case, with the last three months showing clearly his rapid deterioration. We really look upon you as an angel of mercy; since we 'lost' Charger in this way, we've heard many other people's chilling stories of biting dogs.

"This may mark the end of our dog era. Callie has

adjusted pretty well to being an only dog. And it's a relief that the many subtle tensions created by Charger's presence are gone. He did require a great deal of time and energy.

"But we have found there was more pain and grief over his demise than over any other dog we've had. In spite of it all, we miss him terribly. He was a participating family member, and this lovable trait is what people find so endearing in springers. On his last day he was a model of good behavior. Nelson took him for a long walk because he loved the leash. We stayed with him to the end so he wouldn't feel abandoned. He was such a beautiful dog, so strong and healthy. And all the things bred into him to make him strong and healthy also created those monstrous and dangerous seizures. When we knew that, we knew finally his misbehavior wasn't due to our failure to train him. Then we could let go. That's why we consider it most fortuitous that you visited us when you did; you helped to remind us of those vital things."

If you face a similar situation I think you'd find it just as hard to choose euthanasia as Nelson and Barbara Chambers did—especially if you haven't yet tried to correct your pet's misbehavior. Just as in any other euthanasia decision for a pet, you must feel as if you've done everything you can before you authorize the injection. And, like the Chamberses, you'll probably find it as difficult to let go of your problem pet as you would with a well-behaved animal—perhaps more. After all, you acquired and kept him *because* of his lovable qualities and companionship. His behavior problems can never obliterate those positive aspects of your relationship with him. You may feel even closer to this pet if you've spent extensive time working with him; you two have shared a challenge, hopes, and complicated adjust-

ments. If euthanasia does seem your best option after all
that work, you can take as much time as you need to
adjust to *that* choice. It's important to realize other
owners have gone through this confusing emotional experience. Perhaps you'll find someone who understands
your predicament and can reassure you as you make
your decision. Once your incorrigible pet is put to
death, if that's what you choose, you should expect the
same reactions that arise in any euthanasia case: guilt,
relief, and sorrow. I hope that you, too, can realize what
Barbara and Nelson discovered: your pet's dangerous inability to behave is not your fault. If you think he still
has a good chance for rehabilitation, delay your choice;
if not, choose it at an appropriate time for your family
so that you can say good-bye to such a beloved—if
troublesome—friend.

6

Grieving for
the Family Pet

"My daughter, who's twenty-three, is away at college. She doesn't know about Arlo, but I don't think she'd care as much as I do—he seems to annoy her when she's home on vacations. My husband holds it in and thinks about what to do next. My sons are caught up in their plans; they care, but they won't gush over Arlo. Why can't I be that way?"

When you and your entire family arrive at the VHUP with a dying pet, you may think you're acting as a group, with the same motivations and feelings. But as we talk I see one of you reading a bulletin board while another weeps hysterically. Someone else, embarrassed, hunts for tissues and tries to calm everyone. Another kicks the nearest wall. Even if you were all doing the same thing I'd guess that each of you was crying, muttering, or listening for different reasons—and that those varying thoughts might surprise you. You may think of your family as a unit or a group, but that doesn't mean you'll grieve for your pet as one. You're at various ages and in different generations; you have a wide range of experiences, together and separately. You have to consider that others in your family may not react as you do—nor as you expect them to. You must handle each person's feelings and reactions carefully and individually in order to make this shared grief easier for all concerned.

The Bittman family, for instance, came to me after their Lhasa Apso puppy, Candy, had been diagnosed as having a collection of congenital problems that made her barely able to function from day to day. At six months, an age when most puppies seem to grow and play continually, Candy was sickly and stunted. Another pup from the same litter had died just three months earlier; when the veterinarian arrived at the same prognosis for Candy, George and Lena Bittman decided euthanasia would spare the young dog further suffering. Although the choices for the puppy seemed clear, they were confused about how or whether to explain the dog's impending death to their nine-year-old son, Jason. He'd lost two grandparents through death, as well as the other puppy, in the past six months. Every night the boy insisted that the dog sleep at the foot of his bed. George and Lena were sure their son had no inkling of Candy's problems and they wanted to protect him—so much so that they came to see me alone, afraid their tears and worry would scare him.

"Would you tell him for us?" George asked in the middle of our conversation. I let them know right away that breaking the news to Jason wasn't my role or responsibility. I could see they faced a difficult task, I said, in telling their son something they knew would sadden and upset him. I offered to sit in on their conversation with Jason but pointed out that he'd probably value his parents' word more than that of a relative stranger. From their description I knew how much the boy loved his dog and that only their complete honesty would help him come to grips with Candy's impending death.

When all the Bittmans came back to my office for this difficult conversation, it was George and Lena who were shocked rather than Jason. "Of course I want her to live," the boy said, "but I knew a long time ago she was going to die. It seems like everyone's dying, one after the other!" He thought it was unfair that his grandparents and not just one, but two, of his puppies had to die. On the other hand, he had no illusions Candy might live. So the four of us talked about that frustration—about how complicated and unusual the family's feelings were due to their recent series of losses. The veterinarian and I explained euthanasia to Jason. He asked a few questions but seemed to accept the process immediately as Candy's best option. Knowing what would occur in the examination room made him feel better, he said, although he chose not to witness the actual injection. By including him in the decision, the Bittmans found out surprising aspects of his attitudes and feelings and made the experience easier for the whole family.

That session had other interesting results: Jason was intrigued by the thought that Candy's medical problems mystified even the doctors. He asked the veterinarian whether they'd learned anything new from Candy. That led us into a discussion of autopsies and how those post-death examinations sometimes help doctors find clues to new treatments. "Maybe Candy could help another puppy, or lots of puppies, if we asked them to do one," Jason said to his parents. So the family agreed on an autopsy. They also decided to wait to get another dog. Jason did have bad dreams for several nights after Candy was put to death and was quiet and withdrawn both before and after the euthanasia occurred. But he and his parents expected that reaction. When baseball season began a few weeks later, Jason was donning a Little League uniform and returning to his normal nine-year-old routine.

Jason could easily have been a victim of the common instinct to protect loved ones from death. If George and Lena had continued to hide the truth of Candy's condition or had convinced someone else to tell Jason about their euthanasia choice, the boy would have lost a great deal of trust in the people he loved and relied on most. He might have felt the deaths were somehow his fault or been angry and felt isolated at his exclusion from the decision. The Bittmans, like most parents, wanted only to ease the mourning process for him. But their assumptions about Jason's reactions almost made the experience considerably more troubling to the entire family.

That can also happen when adult children try to protect their parents. Rose was a seventy-five-year-old woman whose daughter put her into a position identical to Jason's: no one wanted to tell her her poodle, Tipsy, was dying. Rose's late husband had given her the dog fifteen years before on her birthday, and the Pittsburgh couple enjoyed playing with Tipsy as she advanced from puppyhood. Both Rose and her husband were in their sixties then; she had a problematic heart and he had high blood pressure. One day she went into cardiac arrest and was rushed to the hospital by a neighbor. Her husband, who had been grocery shopping, had a stroke on his way home. He died almost instantly. Because Rose lay in an intensive-care unit battling for her own life after emergency surgery, she didn't hear of her husband's death until well after his burial.

Nearly ten years later Rose had successfully survived that heart attack and resumed a normal life-style, but she'd never been able completely to resolve her husband's death. She wasn't by any means denying her loss, although it had come as a great shock to her. But she did admit that his death would have been easier to accept had she been with him as he died and at his funeral. She compensated for that somewhat with Tipsy, who reminded her of better days and the events the dog had shared with both of them.

Rose wanted to be just as realistic about Tipsy, who seemed to her to be dying slowly but surely. The dog's movements were slow and strained; she ate less and less. Rose always took her to the veterinarian herself and voiced her suspicions, but he kept assuring her Tipsy was just aging normally. In fact, the dog had been dying of cancer for many months. Rose's daughter had heard her concerns about the poodle and contacted the veterinarian. "Please," she begged him, "let me deal with this my way. It'll kill my mother if you tell her the dog's dying, because Tipsy's the only reminder of Dad she has left. I'm afraid the news would bring on another heart attack." So a conspiracy of kindness began behind Rose's back. No one, particularly the veterinarian, wanted to jeopardize Rose's health by mentioning the dog's inevitable death.

Her daughter also called me, hoping I could allay some of her mother's fears for Tipsy. So I called Rose. During our conversation she told me of her suspicions that the dog was extremely ill; she also thought her daughter and her veterinarian were avoiding the truth. "I have another checkup scheduled tomorrow for Tipsy," she told me, "and I know something's wrong. I hate to think that everyone's lying to me, but I'm almost positive that they're holding something back. Tipsy isn't acting at all normally. I don't want to keep her alive and suffering, but I don't want to arrange euthanasia too soon, either. If they keep evading my questions, how will I know what to do? What if she needs treatment? What if she's not comfortable now? I wish they were as worried about my dog as they are about *me*."

I suggested to Rose that she'd have to take the action needed to find out the truth. If she acted as a strong person, asking her veterinarian to help her by disclosing the facts of Tipsy's condition, it might take some pressure off him. She called me the following afternoon to report she had found out how sick Tipsy really was and that she'd decided on euthanasia as the appropriate choice for her poodle. But Rose faced yet another struggle: she wanted to be with her dog at the death and burial. Her daughter opposed her wishes in one last attempt to protect her Rose felt she couldn't live with that—she didn't want to duplicate what had happened when her husband died. "I was left out of his death and his burial, not by my choice," she told me. "I can't bear to be forced out of Tipsy's death too." We talked about the significance the dog's death took on because it symbolized the lost relationship with her husband. When Tipsy died Rose would have to let go of both her husband and her dog, who'd kept his memory alive for so many years. Knowing the truth about Tipsy wasn't enough—she had to witness the death and burial as well, to finally accept the end of those relationships. When Rose explained that to her daughter, adding that she'd feel at risk if she couldn't follow her wishes, she was able to go through with her plans.

Rose was able to change her family's protective actions simply because she was a strong adult. Jason had no such recourse, since he depended on his parents' honesty and guidance. Whenever a family shares the ownership and then the death of a pet, each person deserves special, individual consideration simply because no two family members grieve for identical reasons or in identical ways. Because most families find it difficult to discuss and resolve a pet's death with children, we'll talk about issues for young people later in this chapter. But keep in mind that, like Rose's daughter, you may inadvertently treat an adult as you would a child in this situation. Treating anyone as a child during bereavement is probably more harmful than helpful. Your toddler, your teenager, your spouse, and your parents may all require different levels of explanation—and different types of support. In most cases, however, all family members are entitled to participate in decisions about a pet's death, if that's what they want. Don't assume you know their feelings and thoughts about the pet until you consult them. Again, you may be surprised by the range of reactions you find within your family.

Whose Pet Was This?
Differing Reactions in a Family

Dr. Thompson asked me to sit in on his session with Mrs. Ann Billings one afternoon because he anticipated some problems in their discussion of Arlo, her black housecat. He'd alerted me to the cat's condition two weeks earlier, but Arlo's oral tumor hadn't improved at all. Radiation treatments failed to retard its growth; the veterinarian didn't expect him to live more than two or three months at this point. Because Ann had been upset at the thought of just treating her cat, we thought this latest development might disturb her even further.

I sat with them as Dr. Thompson explained his prognosis for Arlo, watching Ann grow more pale by the minute. Then I interrupted to ask her about what she felt now that she'd heard the cat's condition. It turned out that, like most family pets, Arlo had been acquired for the Billings children, who now ranged in age from fourteen to twenty-three. From Ann's point of view, though, the cat was clearly hers. "I really believe that pets just can't fend for themselves," she said, "and I always feel as if I've let them down somehow when they die. Arlo's *my* responsibility." She had filled in for her children when they forgot or neglected to feed and care for the cat; because the children were busy with schoolwork and friends, she'd spent more time with Arlo recently than they had. Ann was also aware her close relationship with the cat made a euthanasia consideration more difficult. She spoke of the unpleasant experience she'd had when both her parents died two years before and when the family dog had to be put to death the previous year. "I don't want anyone else to decide for Arlo," she told us. "I have to do this; if I hadn't taken the family on vacation to Hawaii, this might never have happened." She explained that the cat first showed signs of trouble within a week of their return from vacation, giving us one reason for the guilt she now felt. Dr. Thompson and I assured her the tumor might have developed months before the family even considered a vacation. We also let her know that a decision could wait. Perhaps Arlo's tumor would at last stabilize on its own. "It's a very slim chance, but waiting will give you time to think it over," Dr. Thompson told her.

"What about your family—how do you feel they'll react to this?" I asked Ann. Her husband, she said, had been most supportive in her distress for Arlo since they returned from Hawaii. "That makes me feel good and bad," she said, "because he wanted to go on vacation without the kids, just the two of us. Maybe I shouldn't have insisted on a family trip. I feel as if this is my punishment." Her sons, fourteen and seventeen, were about to graduate from middle school and high school. "They're thrilled about that, and I want to be happy for them, but this overrides anything else right now," Ann said. "My daughter, who's twenty-three, is away at college," she added. "She doesn't know about Arlo, but I don't think she'd care as much as I do—he seems to annoy her when she's home on vacations." Ann's sister, who lived nearby, had also become involved, chiding her for her lack of emotional control. And Ann herself was frustrated and angry at the way her feelings came spilling out. "My husband can hold it in and think about what to do next," she said. "My sons are caught up in their plans; they care, but they won't gush over Arlo. Why can't I be that way?"

We talked until she calmed herself enough to drive home. I encouraged her to continue to seek support from her husband, since he seemed to be her strongest ally. Of course she'd be upset, I said—wouldn't anyone who loved Arlo so much feel awful about his approaching death? We talked about how difficult it would be to leave the cat in the hospital for observation instead of returning home with him. By the time she was ready to leave, Ann had begun to see that her reactions weren't so strange after all—and that her family's feelings, from indifference to supportive concern, were also natural.

I encouraged Ann to think about whose pet Arlo was. Right now, he was hers. But I reminded her that her children could say the same thing. Although Ann felt responsible for Arlo now, she'd once told her children *they* were in charge of him. To varying degrees he was everybody's cat. Arlo was her husband's newspaper-reading companion, her sons' target for playful teasing, her daughter's major household complaint, and Ann's source of company when no one else was in the house.

Although I can't begin to describe the many different relationships between family members and pets, I can tell you about certain givens that apply to most pet-owning families. Your animal is at least a presence for everyone in the house. Every adult or child finds and develops an individual relationship with the pet almost by default. Whether you relate to the animal negatively or positively, you must have some reaction to him simply because he's a regular fixture in your life. You might think of your pet as a long-term visitor. Someone in the family will probably handle that visitor's needs; another might resent his presence or invasion of your close-knit family life. Someone else will draw strength from the visitor's presence and become his special friend or ally. Perhaps everyone will enjoy having that person around the house.

It's much the same with a pet, except that you *all* own the animal instead of having a social connection to bind you. Your spouse's name may be listed on the official license, but your youngest child may take all responsibility for the pet. Or, as Ann found, adults may buy the animal for the children only to discover themselves spending more time with him. In many families it seems as if different people own the pet at different times. Whoever rises first in the morning might feed the dog and walk him. The child who comes home directly after school might exercise and play with the cat for a few afternoon hours, and another child might feed him after baseball practice. An adult working at home spends quiet hours with the pet nearby; he may not even inter-act with the animal, but he shares those times with him, seeing the happenings others miss when they're at school or an office. Someone else might take the dog along on errands or to a bedroom to get away from the rest of the family. Along with those separate moments there will be times when everyone shares in ownership simultaneously: when the pet accompanies the family on vacation, when he begs scraps at the dinner table, or when he goes from room to room to wake everybody up in the morning. Inevitably, every member of the family talks to the pet as well, whether in confidence or in giving a command.

The best way to discover how the rest of your family feels about your collectively owned pet is through candid conversation. That's particularly useful after a pet has died: you can reminisce together about funny or tragic experiences you shared, tell the others of special times you went through alone with the pet, or simply confess that you didn't care to have the animal around you at all. Try to avoid judging others for feeling differently than you do. Whether they liked, loved, or ignored the animal, their feelings are just as real and valid as your own. As you discover each family member's specific response to the pet, you'll be better able to understand and support those reactions that differ from your own.

Why Children May Handle Grief Better Than Adults

If you're a parent you're responsible to both yourself and your children in any crisis or calamity, so it's natural to want to protect them from trouble, particularly when a much-loved family pet dies. It may be your child's first experience with death in the family—or with *any* death—and therefore you want to handle it carefully.

What concerns me, though, are parents who try to manage their children's grief with too much care. There *is* such a thing as overprotecting children from grief, and it happens often in our society. Few people allow their young children to accompany them to funerals, wakes, or memorial services for deceased friends and family members. Children are rarely involved in sending sympathy cards, expressing sorrow, or other condolence rituals. Many people speak of death in hidden and euphemistic terms, blurring its reality for children. Perhaps that's why so many of us become adults who handle death awkwardly, making inappropriate comments or no comment at all. Most adults think death is far too profound a concept for children to deal with or to comprehend. That may be true, but not by definition. When you brush off their questions with elusive answers, put on a strong front so as not to upset them, or simply exclude them from your feelings and rituals about death, children can usually sense they're being shielded or kept away from the issue. If they don't see you sad or upset they may fear that their own sorrowful feelings are unnatural or wrong. They'll probably wonder even more about what's happening; the details you leave to their imaginations can easily grow out of proportion, giving them false notions about death that you can't control.

I think many children age four or older have most of the resources and logic necessary to confront death directly as well as to work through bereavement. That doesn't mean they won't feel pain, loss, and sorrow—those reactions come as naturally to a child as they do to an adult. Consider, however, the world your child inhabits, the one that will hold him up during this sorrowful time. He doesn't have to socialize or work with adults who are embarrassed about expressing regret and sorrow; he doesn't feel as if he must act maturely and rationally to save face. He knows immediately where to find solace if he needs it—from you. Most helpful of all, a child rarely checks his impulses to cry, scream, stamp his feet, or otherwise vent his emotions. He'll rarely analyze his feelings or wonder whether they're abnormal—if he feels that way, *it's genuine*, unless someone punishes him or shows him more appropriate behavior. He may still choose to follow his first impulse simply because it feels better to do so. Think of how many children scream in church, cry at birthday parties in front of their friends, or automatically lash out at people who anger them. They're less concerned about what others think of them. What's more, most children have some concept of death gleaned from stories, television programs, and their own observations; they've seen insects and stray animals dead or dying outdoors, for instance. They may not fully understand all of death's implications, but they may be far more aware of it than you think.

If adults were more open about death and its attendant emotions, I wouldn't see many grieving owners who struggle with their friends' insensitive comments, their relatives' worries or scoldings, or the many other bereavement problems that stem from society's code of "normal" behavior. In that sense your child is better equipped to cope with a pet's death. Just try him. Open a conversation about the death and listen to his response. If you encourage him to ask questions he will probably be direct and to the point. But remember your child will take some of his cues from you, and you should in turn take some from him. If he wants and needs to talk about his feelings, share yours with him. Don't run away from your child when you want to cry or talk about the pet; he may want to join you, and he'll at least feel assured that crying and emotion in this situation are okay. If you don't share your child's intense grief for a pet, respect and encourage his emotions rather than avoid or ignore him. Ask what you can do for him, even if you can't imagine why a burial or other gesture is necessary.

You may find, as many parents do, that your child doesn't feel as sorrowful as you do about the pet's death. But you can still explain your viewpoint and feelings to him, describing why your relationship with the cat or dog was so important to you and how the loss affects your feelings now. He'll still learn a valuable lesson—that he should respect others' feelings, even when he doesn't agree with or share them.

Occasionally a child will go through an extreme and traumatic reaction to a pet's death. Many parents fail to notice a truly troublesome reaction in a child because the signs are easily mistaken for another problem. Your son or daughter might react in one of two ways: withdrawing completely, preferring to spend more and more time alone, or seeking out companionship every minute of the day, clinging to the nearest relative or friend. Other warning signals of exaggerated grief in children include persistent and violent nightmares, obstreperous behavior where none existed before, continual nervousness or a marked decrease in self-confidence, and a lack of willingness to talk about feelings—*particularly the hesitation to "tell all" to one or both of his parents*. As you can see, none of those signals are clear. You can easily mistake chronic crankiness for a physical illness or childish stubbornness; silence for the natural desire to spend time alone; nervousness for pent-up energy, and nightmares for indigestion. If your child, in his fear of a pet's death, constantly demands your presence, holding onto your hand or crawling into your lap at every opportunity, be alerted. In general, if any of these actions are unusual for your child under normal circumstances, and you notice them during the weeks immediately after a pet's death, you should consider bereavement as a possible cause. It's important, too, to notify your child's teacher when his pet dies; acting up or withdrawal in the classroom can provide just as dramatic a signal that his grief is out of control.

Most often I find that such problems occur in a child as a direct result of the parents' actions. If you minimized the importance of the animal's death, sugarcoated the news, or simply didn't tell your child the full truth about the death, he may feel guilty, confused, and frightened. Many parents tell me they've lied outright to their children when they explain where the pet has gone; among the most common tales are "the dog jumped out of the car and ran away," "the doctor made a mistake and the cat died," or "he just left to be by himself." These "explanations" are more damaging than comforting to a child. Think about what your words say to your youngster: any of those lies could cause your child to think his pet didn't love him after all—that his *own* behavior somehow drove the animal away or that he shouldn't trust doctors and hospitals. If you downplay the pet's death by hiding your own reactions or by denying your child's chances to react naturally and openly, he'll probably leap to the conclusion that something's wrong with him for feeling sad and angry. Worst of all, outright lies such as those about the pet's running away do nothing to resolve a child's grief; instead, they spur both sadness and the futile hope that the animal might someday return, a form of denial that can only be harmful to your child in the long run.

Oddly enough, parents who handle a child's bereavement in this awkward and negligent manner can often recall their own childhood experiences with a pet's death and the ways they were shielded from it. They may, for instance, have been angry when their own parents excluded them from the euthanasia decision for an ailing animal. But they in effect repeat their parents' mistakes in trying to hide the death from children. If you've minimized the death to your child, and he begins to have violent nightmares, resists going to bed or being alone, cries constantly or withdraws from your company, it's a clear signal that, however well-intentioned, you've made the situation worse. The only way to really rectify that mistake once and for all is to sit down with your child and tell him the truth—because the simple facts will hurt him less than the horrors he's begun to imagine. Encourage him to tell you what he's dreaming and thinking and feeling. If he somehow thinks he was responsible for the pet's death, he may have nightmares in which he sees himself directly killing the animal. If you've denied him the chance to participate in a burial or to see the pet's body after death, his nightmares and daytime imaginings might include terrible fantasies about what "really" happened. These are only examples of the possibilities, but I hope they're dramatic enough to persuade you to handle your child's bereavement truthfully.

The other most common reason for a child to react extremely after a pet's death is his relationship with the animal—particularly if the pet has been his one and only friend. The support and friendship of peers is highly important to young children, and many consider their animals to be their "best friends." But if the family pet was your child's sole companion, he must have relied heavily on the animal for comfort, love, trust, and confidence. The pet's death will leave the child feeling completely and truly alone in this instance, so he'll need your honest and supportive help as he struggles to adjust to life without this important friend. This may be a time to consider why your child lacks other relationships on which he can rely. Perhaps you can help alter that situation in some way.

"Was It My Fault?": Handling Children's Questions

Giving your child the time and encouragement to express his emotions won't necessarily resolve his grief quickly. It may bring out more questions than you expected but will do so positively. You're allowing your child to work all the way through his pain rather than shut it off at what seems an acceptable point. As disturbing as it may be to witness your child's hurt, remind yourself that this experience will help him in the future as well as right now.

The most natural questions—"What happened?" and "Why?"—will probably be the first ones your child asks. Your answer depends on his age and level of comprehension. Again, it's important to remember that only children younger than four or five years of age have real trouble understanding death. To them you might simplify your explanation to "He went to heaven" if you know your child has some idea of heaven. But choose your words carefully; telling a small child the animal "went to sleep forever" may prompt him to lie awake every night, afraid to shut his eyes for fear he won't wake up ever again. If your child was fast friends with the pet who died, he may have used that relationship as a basis for comparing his own experiences, as many children do. That comparison may further scare the child if he imagines that he—or you—might die suddenly as his pet did.

Children older than five can be told that the pet has died and what caused the death. Don't worry extensively about taking them through complicated medical explanations; with your encouragement, they'll ask about anything they don't understand. You may want to arrange for them to talk to the veterinarian who treated your pet so they can hear an official explanation of the cause of death. In the case of an accidental death you might want to point out examples that will show children no one is at fault—that accidents do happen. Remind them of wild animals they may have seen dead by the roadside or other instances that will put this kind of random death in perspective for them.

As I did with the Bittmans, I encourage all parents to include at least their older children in a euthanasia decision, if possible, well in advance of the scheduled death. Review with them the issues you've already gone over in your own mind: the veterinarian's prognosis, the cost or effectiveness of further treatment, the animal's quality of life, and your family's quality of life with the pet. Include them in a tour of the hospital or clinic where the euthanasia will occur and ask the veterinarian to explain the procedure he'll use. You should also let them know that this type of death is available only to animals and why; reassure them if necessary that only this particular injection causes death and that others help to prevent it.

After they've received the same information you have about the process, hold a general discussion or speak to each child individually. Ask each one whether he prefers to be present or absent during the injection. Offer your children time alone with the pet before euthanasia occurs so they can say good-bye to the cat or dog if they wish. Most important, talk about your *own* feelings and find out theirs, acknowledging that euthanasia is painless for the pet but painful for the family. I doubt their questions and concerns will be very different from your own.

Sometimes a child will ask something that takes you completely by surprise yet give you clues to his innermost concerns. When a child wonders "Was it my fault? I know I should have walked Barney after school yesterday, but I didn't," you can see why honesty and clarity are so vital in your answers and explanations. Your children are less likely to view the dog or cat's death unrealistically if you're sensitive to their need for the truth—and I think you'll all feel better for having faced the truth together.

Including Children in the Mourning Process

Any child considered old enough to help with a pet's regular care should be able to participate in the decisions and rituals that comprise the mourning process. The choice is the child's. You may want to hold a general discussion or speak to each one individually, but you should offer your children the chance to accept or reject participation.

As you'll see in the next chapter, mourning may be as elaborate or simple as the family wishes. You can involve your children in every step of the process: disposal of the body, settlement of hospital services, memorial arrangements, and special ceremonies. If you don't share your children's need to mourn this loss, you should still pay careful attention to their preferences. Many adults recall the comfort and encouragement they felt when their parents helped them to dig a simple backyard grave or to conduct a special service to mark a childhood pet's death. Years later these people don't consider that their parents may have thought those actions unnecessary. Instead, they focus on the thoughtfulness of the gesture because it acknowledged the validity and importance of their feelings.

You should also make it clear to all family members that those who need time and room to mourn the pet should be respected. Children who don't share a sibling's or parent's sorrow can either comfort the family member or simply avoid him for the time being. You might point out that those who are grieving deeply for the pet probably feel lonely and isolated from the rest of the family right now and that they need more than ever to know their feelings are accepted at home. If you encourage tolerance and kindness in your children as they adjust to a pet's death, they may well thank you someday for treating them like adults during their first bereavement—and they'll have learned early how to deal with that experience effectively.

How Parents and Children Can Help Each Other

Perhaps you and some of your children have just returned from the veterinary clinic where your cat was given a euthanasia injection; you all had a chance to say good-bye to him and the children even held him during the injection. Now, though, they're silent and withdrawn. Or you may have finished burying the dog in your backyard with the help of your children—all except the one who refused to come out of his bedroom. A week may have passed since the burial; you notice that your wife cries whenever she looks outside in the grave's direction and her sorrow troubles you. Maybe you're a member of the family who grew up with the pet but now live several hundred miles away. Your father told you about the pet's death and burial and he sounds more upset than you expected. Is it possible he misses the animal more than you?

Any of those situations, as well as many others, may make you wonder whether someone in your family needs special help to recover from the death. What can you do? Before you take any action I think you should consider the particular relationship that may have existed between the pet and the person who now concerns you. It may be that your father took over the dog's care when you moved away, including him in walks and other activities. Your wife may have spent much more time with the pet, growing accustomed to his company, or she may have taken on his increasing health-care needs just prior to his death. Perhaps she took pleasure in watching the dog run around the yard; now the sight of his grave creates a stunning visual reminder of the enjoyment she's lost. The child who avoided the burial might always have shared his experiences with the pet as they grew up together; now he may delay acknowledging the death because it frightens or threatens him. He might also feel angry, guilty, or depressed. Your children may come home from witnessing euthanasia with many puzzling questions in their minds, even though they asked to be present; their doubts and worries may look like depression and withdrawal to you. Those are just some of the possibilities. If you can't determine the reasons for a family member's reaction to the death, don't assume anything. Instead, talk to your parent, spouse, sibling, or child to hear the reasons only he may know.

It may be more difficult for you to understand those factors if you don't share the other person's intense grief. You may be better able to control your emotions and wonder why one of your relatives seems so out of control. Although his tears, silence, or anger may seem excessive to you, that's only one viewpoint. It's far more helpful for you simply to respect the feelings you don't understand in others at this time. Even in a family no two people have identical reactions, thoughts, or feelings. What's natural and appropriate for one person may be forced and false for another; it's important to make those distinctions and accept them if you want to be of assistance.

I often hear adult women say in counseling sessions that their husbands have great difficulty understanding their intense grief and mourning for a pet. Sometimes the husband grows impatient and frustrated, knowing he's helpless just when he wants most to help. That frustration typically comes out damagingly; he may accuse his wife of "making too much of this" or of "overreacting." Usually I find that men are more embarrassed by an outward display of emotion than by the feeling behind it. The reverse can also be true if a woman expects her husband to remain strong and unemotional during this or any other tense situation. If you find yourself feeling ashamed, angry, or impatient with your spouse—or your children, siblings, or parents, for that matter—*try to be supportive*. You should simply be available to discuss or listen to feelings, to allow for silence and time alone, or any other necessary action. Perhaps you can help that person explore new avenues that will eventually substitute for the time spent with the pet—not just busywork but things that will have special meaning or significance.

If you're away from your family when the pet dies and during the period following, you may want to do what few people consider necessary in this situation— send a card or flowers to the rest of the family or to the person who seems to grieve most intensely. You might have given that person a silent hug and kiss, or a caring look, if you'd been at home. Although flowers and cards can't make up for that physical supportive presence, they will say you understand and accept what your family is going through.

You may want to seek or suggest professional help for a member of your family whose bereavement appears to be more intense or longer in duration than the examples presented here, although you should keep in mind that many people grieve and mourn for a long time after their pets die. It's also important to monitor the reactions of a family member whose physical condition or ailment—particularly heart disease, high blood pressure, or similar conditions—may be affected by extreme emotional responses. At least make sure his prescribed medications are neither neglected nor abused at this time and consult a physician if you observe any adverse reactions. But in general your support, understanding, and compassion will be the most effective contributions you can make.

7
Starting to Cope: Mourning Your Loss

"I'm wondering whether I'm too preoccupied with Boston's burial—I still worry whether he's been buried in the right place, in a grave that's deep enough, in the right kind of box. All those questions kept coming back. . . . I'm counting on what you told me, that this must be part of the normal mourning process. And I hope you'd let me know if I seem to be taking this to an extreme. . . . I think I'm doing better. I'm still angry and sad, but I think that as time keeps going by I'll be able to forget the pain and go on with only pleasant memories."

The letters I receive usually come during pet owners' most troubled times, but occasionally I'll hear from someone who consulted me days, weeks, or months earlier. The owner may wait to write until a new kitten has joined his family or a few days after his dog's funeral—but no matter when he writes again it's usually to describe how he's come to grips with the death. Because I save each person's original letter I can compare the differences in the feelings and concerns they expressed.

Fran, a forty-year-old Louisiana woman, had written

me a distressing letter just after her basset hound, Boston, died of multiple illnesses at age thirteen. The dog's advanced age had brought with it glaucoma, deteriorating teeth and gums, and, finally, kidney failure. Because he'd been this single woman's sole companion for those thirteen years, Boston was a linchpin in her life. His death, a difficult blow in any case, was further complicated because Fran couldn't stay with him when she took him to an animal hospital on New Year's Day. The holiday emergency staff told her she'd be telephoned the next day, a Monday, about his condition. While she was at her office Monday morning, Boston's kidneys failed; the phone call informed her of his death.

Fran's first letter was full of bitterness and doubt. Why had the staff forbidden her to visit Boston until they called? Why hadn't she been more insistent, more assertive? If either of those things had happened, she thought, Boston might not have died alone, without her even saying good-bye.

I'd written to, then called, Fran after that letter arrived, and she told me she planned to bury Boston close to home specifically because they'd been kept apart in his last hours. I thought that sounded like a good start for her mourning process and told Fran the burial might help to put her anger and sorrow to rest. The second letter, sent several weeks later, showed both her progress and her remaining concerns.

"Yesterday I crossed another hurdle," Fran wrote. "It would have been Boston's fourteenth birthday. I spent the day building a flower bed over his grave with the help of my father and some of the neighbors. But I'm wondering whether I'm too preoccupied with his burial —I still worry whether he's been buried in the right place, in a grave that's deep enough, in the right kind of box. All those questions kept coming back while we dug the flower bed, and even that didn't turn out right. I had to start all over to get it where I really wanted it.

"I'm counting on what you told me," she added, "that this must be part of the normal mourning process. And I hope you'd let me know if I seem to be taking this to an extreme. As of now, I think I'm doing better. I'm still angry and sad, but I think that as time keeps going by I'll be able to forget the pain and go on with only pleasant memories."

Fran's second letter did show me she was working through her bereavement, both in what she said and the way she said it. Her first letter showed her many confused emotions at the time of Boston's death: doubt, anger, fear, suspicion. Her second letter even expressed her concern calmly, as if she were finally able to step back from her feelings and look at them realistically. Most important, she was following those feelings, taking productive action to remedy her worries as she saw fit—moving the flower bed was just one good example of the attention she now paid to her own preferences. I was pleased she'd also found supportive people to help her accomplish what she wanted to do. Although she hinted she'd like her recovery to move faster, she knew from our previous correspondence that the healing process takes time. The last line of her letter told me she could accept that.

Fran's concern about Boston's burial, even after it occurred, was by no means an extreme response to his death, but rather a common, appropriate way of resolving her emotions. I wrote her again, saying what I tell every pet owner during the mourning process: it's sensible to choose rituals and memorials carefully because you'll live with those choices once they're made. You should be able to think about the last things you do for that cat or dog—his burial or cremation, his funeral ser-

vice, or other memorials you may select or eliminate
from the process—and feel no regret for your choices.
Fran's meticulous planning would comfort her, easing
the loss of her special companion. Another owner might
prefer to avoid rituals and services, remembering the pet
as he was. But as long as you don't choose a mourning
method that runs counter to your feelings, this process
will help you begin to cope with your sense of loss.

In grief your inner feelings fill your mind; mourning
allows you to give those emotions and thoughts public
expression. Although you can think of it as the last thing
you do for the pet, it's probably as much for your *own*
peace of mind. The dog or cat you've lost through death
may never know whether you buried him under his favorite tree, kept his ashes in a box on a shelf, or did
nothing at all. But you'll carry memories of how you
handled his death with you for a long time, so you must
make choices that will comfort you in the future as well
as right now. Your feelings here should be your guide.

Accepted mourning rituals exist to help you do several things: acknowledge that the death occurred; accept
its finality through palpable and visible actions; pay respect to your pet's memory; and, ultimately, resolve
your grief. At the same time you'll accomplish some
practical matters, including disposal of the body. But
many of the pet owners who consult me during their
mourning are confused about their options. They don't
know what to do and they don't know what's appropriate. If a human family member had died you'd know
almost exactly what to expect from this process. It's
likely a funeral director, with your approval, would assume responsibility for many details related to burial or
cremation. Your religious beliefs, or lack of them,
might guide your choices for or against particular rituals
and actions. As a courtesy, friends and relatives would

probably express their sympathy and regrets in personal visits, cards, letters, flowers, gifts of food, or offers of assistance. A death-absence policy at work might allow you to take a few days off. Bankers, attorneys, and executors would meet to settle the deceased person's estate. Although some people might find it difficult to express their feelings of sympathy, you probably would be spared inappropriate or tactless remarks. (No matter how they feel about a deceased person, most people shy away from "speaking ill of the dead.")

But when a pet dies, owners generally don't know which rituals, if any, apply. When the veterinarian inquires about disposal of the body, many owners ask, "What do people usually do?" If you know precisely which customs you want to follow, you'll still have to rethink each ritual along the way. That's because you can't count on the same acceptance and reassurance from the people around you that you'd have if a human had died. No death-absence policy will cover an animal's death, and you can't expect friends to send cards, flowers, or offers of help. Worst of all, the generally respected taboos against jokes or derisive comments don't apply to pet owners' bereavement. No one would dream of saying "Well, you have two other brothers, so you won't miss this one too much" or "It was only your mother." But pet owners hear similar comments made about their pets during mourning, and those words hurt, as you'll see in the next chapter.

Mourning may be troublesome if you begin to wonder whether such people are justified in their scorn for your rituals and plans. This leaves you open to some extent to questions and disagreements—unpleasant additions to your already distressed situation. Unless you're surrounded by people who support your plans to mourn your pet, you're likely to encounter some resistance to your choices. It's important to remember, however, that *your feelings come first;* although unfortunate, a lack of support shouldn't stop you from carrying out your plans. Pet cemeteries and other agencies are available to help you arrange your pet's burial or cremation, to accept your memorials, and to help you through difficult moments—but the courage of your convictions will help you most of all. You'll see in this chapter that mourning varies from owner to owner, precisely because it's a highly personal matter. I can't make decisions for you. In fact, if you asked me whether you'd made appropriate choices, I'd have to know your feelings first. Some boundaries for accepted mourning rituals do exist, and those limits keep expanding to include new and different preferences. In general, you have as many options for mourning a pet as you would a person.

Making Arrangements for the Body: Your Options

Most people take care of their own funeral, burial, or cremation arrangements well in advance of their deaths, putting their preferences in writing. Obviously, your pet won't do that, but neither will you do it for him; because those arrangements acknowledge death's reality, most people avoid them. If your animal is still alive, but undoubtedly dying, you still may not be ready to accept that death by making plans based on it.

It's never easy to tell someone his pet has died, particularly because that news usually spurs an intense rush of feeling and some difficult decisions. At first your emotions will probably blot out your surroundings and thoughts. Neither I nor any sensitive veterinarian would leave you alone at a time like that, but there's little we can do initially. You may be oblivious to all but two facts: your pet's life is over and your pain is just beginning. So we give you time to adjust. Your immediate reaction will most likely peak and subside in a short while, and it's at that point that I would ask about your preferences for handling arrangements for the body.

You may have only vague ideas here. Even if you always assumed you'd bury your animal in the backyard, for example, you still need to explore other options. You may find that certain city ordinances prevent you from carrying out that burial. Or you may wonder what will happen if you ask the hospital to deal with the body's disposal. It's important for you to pay attention to the limits and options your veterinarian describes and to ask about any procedure you don't comprehend.

In virtually every case of animal death you or the hospital are likely to dispose of the body within twenty-four to forty-eight hours. You need not, however, decide about the method instantly. You should be given the opportunity to consult other family members, if necessary, and to consider the options available. Rarely can or should anyone force you to choose immediately, despite the natural desire to settle such unpleasant matters quickly. You can remind your veterinarian or the hospital staff that these arrangements are important to you, if that's the case, and ask them to give you time to make a decision that will satisfy you. Or you may want to make your choices without delay. In general, you have three or four options from which to choose. Ask about any procedure here that your veterinarian omits from the discussion to ensure you have a complete view of the possibilities.

Private Burials. You're usually able to take your pet's body home for burial on your property, although some limitations may exist. Your veterinarian should know, or be able to find out, whether local laws specify certain depths for the grave, containers for the body, or strictures on grave locations. Burial on private property should be with a sealed container in a grave that's at least three feet deep. This prevents children or roaming animals from inadvertently digging up or coming in contact with the remains; such contact can spread disease and infection.

Local laws aren't the only limits you may face. Frozen ground may make it impossible to dig a grave; tenants on rental property or those who plan to move in the near future may prefer to bury the pet elsewhere to ensure their later access to the grave. If you can legally and practically bury your pet on your property, you're usually responsible for transporting his body from the hospital and can probably claim it almost immediately. It's also possible for the hospital to keep the body until you're prepared for the burial, although this should be as soon as possible after the death.

Private Cremation. Some practicing veterinarians have crematoriums in their clinics or hospitals. At the VHUP we make arrangements with a local practitioner who has one, and your veterinarian may be able to make a similar referral. He may also arrange to have the body transported and the ashes delivered to you afterward or you may prefer to handle those matters.

You should also determine whether the cremation service you choose will guarantee a private, or individual, cremation for your dog or cat. That's why I'm careful about recommending an animal shelter's crematorium, although many of them are available; by unfortunate necessity, many of these facilities handle only mass cremations. It's vital, therefore, that you ask about this detail. I am sure no reputable animal hospital or veterinarian would arrange a mass cremation for your pet if you made another preference known.

Burial in a Pet Cemetery. If you can't arrange for a home burial or a cremation, or don't prefer to do so, you can ask your veterinarian to refer you to the nearest pet cemetery. More than five hundred are estimated to exist in the United States alone; the oldest is the Hartsdale (New York) Canine Cemetery, which has buried more than 40,000 pets since its establishment in 1896. Some pet cemeteries offer a single type of casket and burial plot, with a standard rate that includes all maintenance and service fees. Others provide you with many more options: you may be able to arrange viewing hours, a memorial service, certain types of caskets and plots, grave markers, floral arrangements, and many other details. Costs for labor and materials vary widely throughout the United States, but most pet cemeteries will handle such matters as transporting the body from the hospital as well as the burial.

When the Hospital Handles Arrangements. You may not be able or willing to take care of disposal of your pet's body after his death. Perhaps you're too distraught to go through with a burial or service or your beliefs prevent you from choosing cremation. You may not be able to afford a formal burial in a pet cemetery or be able to bury your pet on your own property. Or you may not choose any of those options, limits or no limits. Remember, no one will force you to choose an option if it's impossible or distasteful for you. Your veterinarian should offer the hospital's services; in general, he will arrange for your pet's body to be transported to a city- or town-operated facility for mass cremation.

Arranging an Autopsy Before Disposal. If your pet's death was caused by an extremely rare disease or physical condition, your veterinarian may request your permission to conduct an autopsy. Or you may want to ask for one if you'd like to know exactly what caused his death when that fact can't be determined otherwise. The process, also known as a post-mortem or a necropsy, may allow your veterinarian to learn more about that specific fatal condition and its potential for cure.

I want to reassure you that, in my experience, veterinarians don't suggest autopsies because they enjoy doing them; the case must have some educational and medical value. Many times there's no reason for an autopsy; to qualify, your pet is likely to have had a particularly baffling or unique illness. At the VHUP, a teaching hospital connected with a veterinary school, autopsy results are used in training veterinary students and doctors, so I wouldn't discourage one of our doctors from approaching you about this matter, although the final choice is always yours.

Of course you're not likely to request an autopsy until or unless your pet has died or is about to die—a time when you may have trouble even contemplating his death, let alone the thought of someone tampering with his body. You might also worry that an autopsy will interfere with your plans for burial or cremation. That's not necessarily true. As he explains the procedure your veterinarian should tell you about cosmetic autopsies: the doctor performs surgery on the body to remove one or more organs that he wishes to study, then stitches the opening so the body is presentable for burial. If a more extensive autopsy is necessary, the remains can still be cremated and the ashes returned to you, if you prefer.

I hope your veterinarian will acknowledge how difficult your loss and this decision will be if he requests an autopsy. As with any arrangements, you should have an opportunity to consider the situation before you decide. Sometimes it's obvious immediately that you can't bear to allow it and you should make that clear if your veterinarian doesn't recognize your objection. He should, in any case, thank you for considering his request; it's a service to the veterinary profession that only you can authorize.

You may want to know why your veterinarian thinks the autopsy will help his work; he should share that information and the autopsy results with you if you want to know. He can tell you when he expects to have conclusive findings, and you may want to contact him at that time if you haven't heard about the results.

"She's Gone, but She'll Never Be Forgotten"

When you mourn you attempt to put your relationship with your pet into words and actions that will, in the long run, help you to accept his death. There are as many ways to do that as there are pets and owners, and no one can say your specific mourning rituals are right or wrong. You choose the framework for mourning once you've made arrangements for your pet's body, but the decisions you make after those plans are in motion can make this process even more unique and helpful.

Mike, a thirty-six-year-old accountant living in Oregon, helped his Saint Bernard, Miss B, through a long, painful illness. When she died he had her body cremated and the ashes placed in an urn. He suspected he might move several times for business reasons and he wanted to make sure that some memorial to their companionship would accompany him wherever he went. In the meantime the urn had a place of importance in his apartment. "It's surrounded by my favorite pictures of her, along with her leash, her favorite ball, and some of her collars and tags. She's gone, but she'll never be forgotten," he assured me in a letter.

I doubt Mike would forget Miss B even without that

collection of reminders, but putting them together probably gave him a chance to think about her and to express
his feelings. I can imagine he spent at least a couple of
hours sifting through stacks of photographs from each of
their eight years together, looking for those that brought
back the most vivid memories. He may have had to fer-
ret the ball from behind the couch or ransack a closet for
those old tags and collars. Those simple tasks were part
of his mourning for Miss B, turning up painful and
pleasant memories as well as physical reminders. The
final arrangement of those items might have taken only
a few minutes and a few inches of shelf space, but Mike
knows that his small tribute to his dog is just as he wants
it—permanent and portable, always available to provide
satisfaction and comfort. Any visitor to his apartment
who notices the reminders will see Mike's devotion to a
beloved pet.

Fred and Gerry McCullough, a couple in their late
twenties, went through the same process in the opposite
way. Instead of displaying their mementos of life with
Plum, their purebred Siamese, they systematically
stored all her belongings after she was killed in a car
accident at age nine. "Neither of us wanted to throw her
things away," said Gerry, "but even the sight of a catnip
mouse would start me sobbing. I have trouble remembering to avoid the pet-food aisle in the supermarket,
and that's hard enough. So we hid everything, piece by
piece."

"But even that took all day to do," added Fred. "I
found a picture of Plummer taken on the day she came
home with us from the breeder. She was so small then
she could hide behind the toaster! We talked about almost every single thing we found—her show ribbons,
her collars, her special toys. It was a relief to put them
away, but we took pains with the boxing up and the

packing. It turned out to be nice to get the memories going for a little while."

You may decide to put your pet's photograph in a place of honor or in a drawer; keep his bed in the attic or give it to a new pet owner you know; throw away his food, leashes, and dishes, or donate them to your local animal shelter. You may want to make a donation to your veterinarian, animal hospital, shelter, veterinary school, or pet cemetery in your animal's memory. One of the monetary donations received at the VHUP came from a twenty-seven-year-old New Jersey woman whose bulldog, Jack Daniels, had died in our emergency service after a poisoning accident. Mary didn't ask us to specify the donation in Jack's name; instead, she wrote, "Just say it's in memory of a dog who gave his owner seven years' worth and more of love and happiness!"

That appreciative attitude is just one reason why pet owners often design special mourning rituals to help themselves through bereavement. The donation of equipment and money or the careful packing of a pet's belongings signify the animal's value to you and perhaps your concern for other animals. Whether you spend hours wondering which method best suits you and your memory of the pet or move swiftly and with conviction, you're beginning to acknowledge he was a special friend. That means your grief and mourning, as well as your appreciation, are justified. Would you do these things if you hadn't cared for the animal? I doubt it. As much as it may hurt to realize your pet can't be with you anymore, it helps to express your respect and love for him—whether you do so only in your mind or with many people around you. In the confusing mix of emotions you experience during grief you might worry that, somehow, someday, you'll forget how wonderful your pet was. Even though that's not likely to happen, taking action to ensure his memory may provide you with stability and reassurance as you learn to accept your feelings.

In addition to those smaller parts of the mourning process, you may want to recognize your pet's worth and importance formally. That's why so many burial and cremation rituals have developed, and if you've chosen one you can control most of the details that will make it much more than a method of disposal. As you dig a small grave behind the house, watch the cemetery staff lower the casket into the ground, or place the urn of ashes on a shelf, you can see and sense your pet's death clearly and powerfully. That striking realization carries comfort because you've surrounded it with gestures of respect and dignity. Whether you handle those rituals all by yourself or turn them over to professionals, you know they're done with the special care and thoughtfulness your pet deserves.

Formal mourning rituals may also encourage you to resolve your own reactions and feelings. If you were overcome with guilt or anger because you couldn't prevent your pet's death or couldn't be with him when he died, you may find that you can begin to settle those feelings as you plan and carry out his burial or cremation with the utmost care. I've seen many grieving owners override their depression as they become involved with a ritual. Most important, you'll find it difficult to continue denying or delaying acceptance of his death after you've seen his ashes or his body; the urn or grave serves as a real and constant reminder that he's indeed dead, allowing you to mourn rather than hold back your emotions.

You may find that a ceremony or service, with or without burial or cremation, provides you with a designated time to focus on your pet's death and to express your sorrow. If you choose to bury your animal in a pet cemetery, a special area or room is usually available for the service; you can choose a simple, standard set of words provided by the cemetery and spoken by one of its staff. Many people rely on their own religion's conventions for such a ceremony, and some ask their ministers, rabbis, or priests to officiate or attend. Perhaps you'd prefer to make this occasion even more personal by preparing and writing the farewell yourself. Whether it's set in the backyard, the cemetery, or some other place, it's wise to include only those aspects of a service with which you feel comfortable.

Sometimes I get glimpses of how these rituals are conducted. Pet owners have sent me poems they've written to be read at an animal's funeral or copies of essays written by others that seem special and appropriate to them. I hear about flowers planted or placed on the grave, ashes scattered over yards and gardens, special markers and inscriptions that create permanent memorials in cemeteries. Eulogies are sometimes written and read by the owner or a clergyman, or the family may have a simple but special discussion about their memories of the pet during his burial. At the end of this book you'll find two essays written specifically for bereaved adult pet owners. The first, written by magazine and newspaper reporter Bill Shaw, describes how Lady, his Irish setter, met with an accidental death that brought out her owner's surprising and conflicting feelings— emotions he feels have shaped his subsequent relationships with pets, helping him to better understand their value. The second, by playwright and author Eugene O'Neill, speaks in the voice of his favorite Dalmatian, Blemie, after the dog's death; it offers the pet's legacy to his owner.

If you don't want to go through with a special ceremony, service, burial, or cremation for your pet, I think you should still feel as if you can think and talk about your memories and emotions, taking advantage of simpler ways of mourning. Even the act of authorizing someone else to handle arrangements and cleaning out your pet's belongings will help you do that. You can't avoid the process if you wish to deal with your loss effectively; many objects and possessions will remind you of your pet and you'll be better prepared to handle the memories if you establish and express them from the outset.

Looking for Support as You Mourn

Because it begins immediately after you discover your pet has died, the mourning process and its necessary decisions are particularly difficult. You have to cope with your feelings, necessary arrangements and payments, and others' reactions simultaneously. That would be strenuous for almost anyone, so it's important to consider on whom you can rely for support and advice.

Your veterinarian can and should be a vital source of support. He's responsible not only for the information and circumstances regarding your pet's death but for helping you to understand what arrangements are available. With him you may discuss and settle how to transport and dispose of the body, payments for services provided before and after the death, and other procedures, such as autopsies. He should provide you with all the time, encouragement, and information you require to accomplish those things in a manner you won't later regret. He may also be the first person who can offer you concern and comfort. Ideally, I shouldn't have to intervene in this cooperative effort between you and your veterinarian; the start of the mourning process is his domain and responsibility, the final step in his services to you and this pet.

Some veterinarians have, unfortunately, not been able to accomplish these tasks efficiently or effectively. Your veterinarian may handle this crucial discussion awkwardly, perhaps not taking it as seriously as you do. At this time, when your grief is probably at its most intense, you don't need to hear his judgments on the value of pet cemeteries, that cremation is too troublesome to arrange, or any other personal biases he may have about the process. Unless you request an option that is illegal or truly impossible, there is no reason for him to tell you what's appropriate. If that happens I recommend you remind him how important these decisions are to you. That's reason enough for him to comply with your wishes. Naturally it's distressing to discover your pet's doctor doesn't support you at this time, but I think you'll have more trouble resolving your feelings if you go against your own wishes. Remember, too, that you're in a position to authorize or deny any part of the process, from autopsies to burial arrangements.

That also applies to your dealings with a pet cemetery or crematorium staff, although I'd expect any of these professionals to respect and understand your bereavement. You can always take your business elsewhere if you find practices and attitudes that may complicate your mourning. Establishing that your decisions are of importance to you personally is, again, the most effective way to maintain your control. It's encouraging that many animal-health professionals now acknowledge the difficulty of pet-owner bereavement with a personal phone call, a sympathy card, or some other gesture of condolence.

Among the other arrangements you must settle with these professionals is payment for services. If your veterinarian or the pet cemetery staff doesn't initiate that subject, you should. You may already have a running estimate of costs, particularly if your animal had been treated for some time prior to his death. Ask about the final fee assessment, including transportation, holding, or cremation of the body. When you choose from the options available at a pet cemetery, ask for costs as the discussion progresses so you can better make your final decisions. Few professionals feel comfortable talking about money when you're still experiencing the first of your bereavement reactions. However awkward they may feel, it's important for both of you to settle the matter as soon as possible so you can go through the mourning process without that added concern.

Naturally, you will want to tell your family and friends about your pet's death, just as you'd inform them of any important event in your life. Be prepared, however, for reactions that may surprise you. As you'll see in the following chapter, you can cope with negative and unexpected reactions in a way that allows you to continue with your healing process. But you may also know a number of other pet owners—people whose shared experience with animals makes them more sympathetic to your situation. *Seek them out as an important support resource*. Whether you work with someone who keeps birds or fish, know the neighbors who walk their dogs around your block every night, or stay in touch with the breeder who sold you your cat, you have a vital network of understanding people on whom you can rely. Remember, too, that choice of breeds and other differences between you and other pet owners don't really matter at a time like this: a person who prefers birds or cats can still support and encourage you during your grief for a dog because he cares about animals and knows intimately what it's like to include one in his life.

I think most animal owners have at least briefly imagined—and then dismissed—the horrible feelings they'd have if their pets died. It's a situation all owners dread, often unknowingly, so they're more likely to accept your emotional responses as normal and appropriate. Perhaps these will be the people who can best help you to make decisions during this time, offering advice and comfort based on their past experiences with animals. You may even find similar encouragement from someone who doesn't currently own a pet but has had an animal at some time in the past—one so special the owner couldn't bring himself to acquire another pet. That doesn't change the way he's always felt about animals, and it certainly means he'll understand the pain *you're* experiencing. It's just as important to seek out these truly sympathetic people as it is to avoid those who don't understand the bonds between you and your pet.

8

Dealing with People Who Misunderstand Your Bereavement

"When he heard me crying, his comment was, 'Come on, Eve, it was only a cat!' I felt like screaming. I was so furious, I slammed down the phone and haven't spoken to him since. How could he say that to me? He'd been a very close friend, but no more, after that reaction!"

After working with hundreds of bereaved owners I can see how difficult it might be for others to express their condolences after your loss. You may be angry, inconsolable, ambivalent, or severely depressed; many of those reactions are difficult to detect. What's more, nothing I can say will reverse the death or change your feelings about it, and you may find that as frustrating as I do. So I usually wait to respond to your grief until I can take some cues from you; if you tell me how you feel or in what way you're most upset, I'm far less likely to make an inappropriate remark.

I've also seen that even a single negative comment about your grief, particularly from a family member, relative, or close friend, can deepen your anger and sorrow. That's what happened to Eve, although most of her friends and family were sympathetic when her twelve-year-old cat, Sidney, died from cancer of the liver. Sidney's death came as a surprise to Eve and her six-year-old daughter; they'd lived alone with Sidney ever since Eve's divorce five years earlier and had never seen him sick.

"I wasn't prepared for it," Eve wrote to me, "and neither was my daughter. She doesn't understand yet what death means, and so we're both having a hard time accepting Sidney's death. It was my first real encounter with death—I kept feeling for a heartbeat, a pulse, anything, and then I ran to the clinic with her because it was so hard to believe." Eve arranged for Sidney's burial at a nearby pet cemetery; two days after the cat's funeral her best friend happened to call.

"When he heard me crying, his comment was, 'Come on, Eve, it was only a cat!' I felt like screaming. I was so furious, I slammed down the phone and haven't spoken to him since. How could he *say* that to me? He'd been a very close friend, but no more, after that reaction!" she wrote.

So Eve added an intense anger to her feelings of shock and hopelessness. When she wrote me a few weeks after the phone call she still had trouble reconciling the death. "I can't get it out of my mind," she wrote, "and my daughter still talks about him every day. I feel so hopeless and I miss him so much!"

It's obvious Eve's friend saw Sidney's death from a completely different perspective, a natural occurence since the bereavement process is so highly personal. But just as Eve did, you may hope or expect that your family and friends feel as you do about your pet's death. From my experience I think you'd be extremely lucky for all or most of them to respond that way. They may be unprepared for your news and their surprise may spur immediate and inappropriate comments. The person who offends you may not have the same values, attitudes, and feelings you have, particularly about pet ownership. Many people have never had a special relationship with a cat or dog, and even fewer with birds, reptiles, or rodents; some fear animals, are allergic to them, or just don't like them. Others may consider pets belongings rather than family members. Don't people, for obvious reasons, refer to themselves as pets' owners rather than their relatives? You may think of the animal as much more than a possession because you've experienced interactions the importance of which others can't possibly understand. The affection, trust, support, companionship, and love that have developed between you and your pet over time aren't usually obvious to other people; they may have no idea of his importance to you. It's possible your family or friends may respond inappropriately just because they have trouble accepting and acknowledging death and your reactions to it.

Unfortunately, another person's negative response to your grief may hurt you just when you need and are seeking crucial support for your feelings. Bereavement places you in an extremely vulnerable position; the death, and its effect on you, may leave you wondering whether you've lost control of your emotions as well as having lost your pet. It's natural for you to seek comfort from your relatives and friends because their encouragement and acceptance at this time would signal that your other relationships won't change even though your friendship with your pet is over. Their understanding also helps you to see that your reactions are normal, natural, and allowable. If, however, they react in a way that hurts or surprises you, it may be difficult to muster enough control to view their behavior rationally. You may consider their words a personal affront, an attack on your pet, or simply callous. Your reaction to their comments and actions may surprise them as well—perhaps, as Eve did, you now refuse to speak to your best friend or just feel uncomfortable in his presence.

Eve, for instance, might have taken the time to explain to her friend that Sidney had been an important source of comfort to her after her divorce and during the years when she had to raise her daughter alone. I can't say whether that explanation would have changed his reaction, but it might have prompted him to choose his words more carefully. At least he would have had more information about her feelings and a better sense of what she considered appropriate under the circumstances. Eve might have found out that her best friend just didn't like pets or that he didn't see them as important—a clear signal she should look for wholehearted support elsewhere. In the same way you may be able to find out how your friends and relatives can say things, or not say things, that hurt you, perhaps unintentionally. A rational examination of their responses can help you to deflect much of the anger and hurt you may feel for them, making your bereavement less stressful and agonizing.

This chapter will look at the negative reactions I hear pet owners discuss most often, as well as some of the points of view those responses express. After you've considered others' viewpoints and attitudes, it's also important to look at your *own* response to these negative comments; in many cases your own anger may cause the most serious disruption of the bereavement process.

"Why Don't You Just Get Another One?"

Bonnie and Phil, a retired St. Louis couple in their sixties, had owned Pekingese dogs for as long as they could remember. The first, Jo-Jo, lived to be fifteen years old. When she died in her sleep one night they returned to a local breeder and bought another Peke within days of her death. "Both of us found the silence around the house unbearable," wrote Bonnie, "and since we'd both stopped working a couple of years before Jo-Jo died, we decided we needed a dog's company. Of course, Timba was nothing like Jo," she added. "But we enjoyed her for herself. She followed me all over our small house every day, and she'd go on long walks with Phil every evening."

Timba, however, wasn't to live as long as Jo-Jo did. "We honestly thought she might be our last pet when we bought her," admitted Phil when I called the couple. "After all, Bonnie and I aren't getting any younger, and our Pekes have always lived a long time." But Timba's heart failed one morning in the kitchen while Bonnie was in another room and Phil was outside. "When I walked in and saw her lying on the floor, so still and quiet, I almost couldn't believe it!" Bonnie wrote. "I called Phil from there—I couldn't even move from where I stood. She was just five years old, and we had no idea she was failing."

Bonnie and Phil were so taken aback by Timba's death that they asked the hospital to handle the body's disposal for them after an autopsy was conducted. But they had further surprises to face: although they felt sure they couldn't bear to acquire another Peke, their children assumed they would. "I couldn't seem to explain enough to them that Timba's death was just too hard for us to handle," Phil said. "They probably thought another dog would help, since it had before, but this was different for us—Bonnie and I didn't want to take another risk like that. It wasn't fair that Timba died so young, and it wouldn't be fair to try to replace her. We had just changed our attitudes."

Unlike some of the other reactions you face, the words "Why don't you just get another one?" may indicate a genuine concern for your recovery, discomfort at your unhappiness, a desire to help end your grief, or ignorance about your deceased pet's importance. Certainly, Bonnie and Phil saw that their children's remarks were well-intentioned and expected, since they had been helped before by buying another dog soon after Jo-Jo's death. They didn't question the couple's affection for Timba, or at least they probably didn't mean to do so. To them it seemed logical that Bonnie and Phil could once again resolve their mourning by starting a new relationship.

Unfortunately, anyone who makes this remark hasn't grasped a vital point: no relationship is replaceable. Friendship builds and develops over time; needs and interdependencies grow for reasons only the participants seem to understand. That's why bereavement, or any other end to a relationship, takes time to resolve. You won't spend five years getting over a five-year relationship, but you shouldn't expect to come to grips with the loss immediately, either. What's more, you may find that resolution of feeling even more difficult to reach if you begin another, similar relationship before your period of grief has ended. You may feel it's disrespectful to the deceased pet to acquire another so soon, or at all; even if you did get another pet you'd likely find yourself making some comparisons. You might resent the new pet for behaving differently from the one you were accustomed to. That's not the best way to start any relationship—the new cat or dog can't possibly live up to the expectations created by his predecessor. You may like the animal you acquire during your bereavement but he still may represent something negative: he probably wouldn't be with you if your other pet weren't dead. You may wish you had the previous one instead. So your commitment to another pet at this time may be ambivalent and unsteady at best if you don't acquire him willingly. At worst, premature commitment to another pet may make you feel uneasy, perhaps adding more anger and guilt than you should expect under the circumstances.

Sometimes your friends or family members don't just suggest another pet to ease your grief, but actually buy or adopt one for you. I think that carries their assumptions about your need for companionship too far, if the action doesn't reflect your preferences. It may also seem the best way to ease *their own* discomfort in handling your bereavement. Some of the pet owners I counsel insist on having another pet immediately, as Bonnie and Phil did after Jo-Jo's death. If that's your own choice, made without pressure from others, you can probably take home that new pet without worry. But when someone shows up at your door with an animal under his arm, you should make it clear that though you appreciate the thoughtfulness of the gesture you're simply not yet ready to have another. It's most important for *you* to make decisions for yourself right now. Even if you find it difficult to turn down an adorable pet that might not otherwise find a home, you should accept it only if it's the pet you want in your home. It would be more helpful, not to mention courteous, for your family or friends to inquire about your interests, needs, and preferences first. If they assume they know what's best for you at this time, make a point of correcting their assumptions with a straightforward explanation of your feelings. Let them know you need time to get over the first pet's death, if that's how you feel, or that you can't bear to consider a new pet so soon. Turning down the gift and the good intentions behind it may offend your family or friends but that's not necessarily your problem. Trust yourself to know what's appropriate for your situation and make sure that's clear to the people around you. As Bonnie and Phil discovered, you may not choose to handle this bereavement for a pet as you did previously, and no one will understand that change of mind better than you.

If the pet who died wasn't the only animal you owned, you may hear another version of this comment: "Well, you have another dog—you won't miss him so much." Again, though it may comfort your friend or relative to think your feeling of loss will be easier with another cat or dog in the house, you may have to remind that person—and yourself—that no two relationships are alike. Marta, a twenty-seven-year-old Californian, wrote me that her family owns "three dogs, two cats, a gerbil, a parakeet, and five goldfish—and each one has a distinct personality and a special place of its own in our hearts. We say that some of the pets are mine, my husband's, or that they belong to each of our children, but they really stand out as individual characters to all of us." You may feel the same way about your pets. Although it may well reassure you to have one or more animals around when another dies, none of your pets can, or should, replace the one you've lost. It's possible that others haven't considered how individually important each pet has become in your life, and you may want to explain it that way.

"Oh, Come On—It Was Only a Pet!"

Eve's tears, heard over the phone by her friend, prompted this comment, but you don't have to be crying or openly upset to bring it on. Some hear it when they request a day or so off from work to get a handle on their feelings, when they tell a friend they've planned a pet's burial, or explain their sorrow and social withdrawal as a response to the death. This particular comment can affect your feelings on many levels, but it's likely to anger you at first, as it did Eve. It doesn't just attack your demeanor during your grief but implies that you should neither feel what you do feel nor recall your close, caring relationship with the pet.

If Eve had told you what she described in her letter to me, I think you'd find it difficult to tell her that Sidney was "only a pet." She spoke of him this way: "He slept by my bed every night; now, I miss that secure presence. I'd had Sidney with me since he was just three months old, and I felt as if I'd lost a child. He comforted me during the breakup of my marriage and in the difficult years that followed, always there for me to hug and cry with when I needed someone. Having an animal so totally loving and sweet for so long was a great support for me."

Even if you haven't yet thought about all the reasons for your pet's role and significance in your life, I think you'd probably react as strongly as Eve did if your feelings were denied in this way. It may hurt all the more to hear those negative comments from someone who knew or knew about the pet before his death; it's natural to expect someone who knew of your affection for your pet to be sympathetic. What's more, you may be able to dismiss one person's remark as insensitive and misguided, but when several people say "It was only a pet" you're likely to feel at once troubled and confused. To you, grieving and mourning the animal seem not only appropriate but natural—feelings you couldn't deny even if you tried. When others contradict your reactions you may start wondering whether your sorrow is silly, unusual, or an overreaction—doubts that may convince you to hide your feelings and be ashamed rather than expressing what you feel and coping with the responses to loss.

Sometimes this reaction is expressed by another person's laughter or the words "Don't you think you should be over it by now?" No matter how the people around you express disapproval of your intense attachment, you must realize that they're insensitive, embarrassed, ignorant, or all three. Perhaps you can determine how they feel about pets: Do they see animals as possessions, childish playthings, or a waste of time and money? Do they simply dislike animals? Or is it that they are really uncomfortable with death and with your distraught reaction? It's likely that the person who says "It was only a pet" has never had an animal companion or never cared much for any pets they had. This means that you two work from completely different backgrounds and experiences. Again, that doesn't excuse callousness or opinionated remarks, but it may soothe you to realize that someone simply doesn't understand your situation.

Of course if you're convinced your pet was indeed a special friend, you can remind yourself that you know better. Think about the times you shared with your animal, the companionship that grew between you over the years. If others' remarks cause you to doubt that bond and its worth, sort out the different levels of comfort you found in your pet's company—prove to yourself that he was vital and worthy of the sorrow you now feel.

You may think you've done something wrong to bring out such dubious comments from your friends, but I'm sure that's not true. No one can foresee another's reaction completely, and I doubt you'd do anything to prompt negative feelings in your friends.

When someone belittles both your relationship with and your grief for a pet, your best recourse is to ignore the remark or laughter if you can. You'll find it difficult, if not pointless, to try to explain that you see the comment as rude, unfeeling, or inappropriate; the person you chide will only become defensive, even hostile. Walk away from it, end the phone conversation, or try to forget the note that expressed this negative response. Once you've said "No, this pet was important to me" and found that your friend still doesn't understand, it's extremely difficult to reeducate him. Attempting to correct his error may only serve to upset you further.

"Well, That's One Less Thing to Worry About"

Shari's schedule was undoubtedly busy; she and her husband both worked full-time and were raising two children. Her job at a Delaware chemical company involved client relations in distant cities; from time to time she made long-distance business trips that took her away from home for several days at a time. Her elderly parents lived only minutes away from her home, and because they could no longer drive, she spent many nights and weekends doing errands for them or taking them to their respective doctors for checkups and medical care. But her family also included Hoosier, a calico cat who'd strayed into her garage eight years ago; when Hoosier developed diabetes, Shari added visits to the veterinarian to her already crowded schedule. "We would have done anything to help that cat," Shari said, "because he'd been so loving and entertaining for the children and for us. Sure, sometimes I had to juggle appointments just to take him in for a simple checkup, but I owed him that care."

When Hoosier died Shari couldn't hide her despondency at the office, although she continued to do her work. One of her assistants, who knew how busy she was, remarked that Shari "must be relieved—after all, you had enough to do without hauling that cat to the veterinary clinic every week! It's one less thing to do."

Shari could barely control her anger. "I didn't say anything, because I had to supervise this person every day. But I despised her attitude! If she was trying to make me look on the bright side, it didn't work—Hoosier's death relieved his discomfort, but there was no bright side to it in our family. I really wondered how she could speak of an animal as if he were nothing more than a briefing statement that I could file and forget!" she said.

I've seen many pet owners whose lives include numerous activities and obligations in addition to caring for dogs or cats, or both. Often their pets take on an extra-special value simply because they must go to great lengths to accommodate the animal in their hectic lives. These owners make time willingly, recognizing the benefits they'll receive in return for their efforts. A busy executive may relish a cat's soothing company after a long day of meetings and phone calls; a working mother might appreciate a pet because he keeps her children entertained and also greets her at the door when she arrives home. The owner in this situation rarely sees the animal as yet another item on a "to do" list; were that the case, the pet probably wouldn't be part of the person's high-powered life.

Others who respond with the same indifference may, however, have heard you refer to the pet only as part of a series of scheduled duties: "Today I've got the craziest schedule—I have to run Jody to the dentist's on lunch hour and be back for a client meeting at 1:00, and then I have to finish the project report in time to get Amber to the animal hospital before 5:00, and get home in time to fix dinner." Then the misunderstanding may be easier to understand, if not accept; you can perhaps correct it by explaining how much reassurance and comfort the animal provided, giving the offending person a more intimate view of your life involving the animal. It's also possible such a person holds some of the differing viewpoints about animals I've already mentioned—fear, dislike, or ignorance of pets and how they can be important to certain people. Again, you know the truth and the circumstances much better than any other person could, and you should take comfort in that knowledge.

The Benign Response: When Someone Says Nothing

When you tell someone—an office associate, a friend, or a relative—that your pet has died, and that person doesn't respond at all, it may seem as painful as if he'd actually said the death was insignificant. What's more, you have no clues to his true feelings. He might not consider a pet's death worthy of comment or he might care considerably but feel he lacks the right words to say something helpful. In this case even a negative response would seem more helpful to you if it were genuine; then you'd at least be able to determine whether he supported or denied your grief. But you can expect to have difficulty dealing with someone whose thoughts and feelings remain unknown to you.

That's why you may want to ask what he's thinking and assume he understands neither your feelings nor what to say to console you. Many pet owners have told me that they say "I wish you'd say *something!*" when faced with a wall of silence. Often the other person will reply "Well, I don't know what to say." At least that tells you your friend or acquaintance isn't oblivious to the death, its significance to you, and your bereavement. Perhaps that's the best you can hope for in this situation. Remind yourself that responding to another's grief is a task most people handle awkwardly and that this person may not intend his silence to hurt you. If your questioning uncovers a negative reaction your friend was trying to keep from you, you can adjust accordingly by dropping the subject and walking away.

Falling into the "Poor Me" Syndrome: Redirected Bereavement

As you've seen, no simple or completely adequate solutions exist to remedy the negative responses you may face during the bereavement for your pet. I don't feel entirely satisfied telling you to avoid confrontations, since I know your emotions are important to you. Perhaps, as many owners do, you don't want to disguise or lie about your feelings; you may want to be open and honest about them, despite the risk of negative or belittling responses. But I wonder whether you really believe that explaining and arguing your feelings will make a difference. While you may hope to change someone's opinion or outlook on pets—and particularly your special pet—you should realize from the outset that your aims are probably impossible to achieve. You don't have to *prove* anything to anyone. You are entitled to care for your pet, entitled to grieve and mourn, and nobody has the right to make judgments about those feelings.

Your determination to confront others directly can lead to more than just awkward situations. You may, after several rebuffs or negative remarks, start to feel sorry for yourself, and self-pity won't ease or help the situation. If you let a "poor me" attitude develop it can misdirect your anger, sorrow, guilt, and depression into blame for those who have hurt you.

It's almost too easy to fall into the "poor me" syndrome, particularly because you can get more attention from others if you present yourself as a victim of cruelty and thoughtlessness. But that kind of pity, or any other pity you receive from other people, won't make you feel any better, either—it just reinforces the dangerous cycle you've started for yourself. While you commiserate with others or rationalize your self-concern, you're liable to distort reality; you may find you are no longer focused on what is at the core of your feelings, which is your pet's death. You cannot work through the healing process if your emotions are not in a proper perspective and related to the loss and separation. That's why I caution so many pet owners not to feel sorry for themselves. It's one thing to seek my help in coping with others' negative reactions; it's quite another to turn this natural healing process into anger directed at others for exaggerated or inaccurate reasons. Such behavior can be as problematic as excessive denial or any other extreme reaction. You risk closing down important relationships with others over what may be small misunderstandings and you are likely to redirect your energy into fighting with others instead of trying to help yourself.

The only effective way to feel better about your pet's death, and to finally put it into an acceptable perspective, is to work through your own feelings. Don't excuse those feelings based on the inappropriate remarks of others. Unfortunately, humans will always be naive, unaware, uncomfortable, and sometimes uncaring about death and the sorrow of others; many avoid the subject, make light of it, or fail to see it in a realistic perspective. That doesn't mean that such people are villains, evil, or inhumane. Nor does it mean that you're exempt from encountering people with those attitudes. These situations are both difficult and common for almost everyone who's experienced grief and mourning after the death of a pet.

If you're beginning to feel victimized by negative remarks from others about your behavior at this time, it's important to consider your attitudes as well as theirs before you continue to act in ways that make your struggle even harder. Remind yourself, too, that you'll only make yourself feel worse if you dwell on others' reactions and your subsequent hurt just at a time when you should by trying to help yourself feel better. By directing your attention to resolving your *own* feelings about the pet you lost you'll be better able to cope with yourself and others.

9

How to Resolve Your Bereavement

"Getting another dog right now would be the same thing as saying that Woody wasn't all that special to us, and that's just not true. Right now we're lonely because we'd rather have him with us, not because we just want any old dog. When we're ready we'll get another one."

My office sits just beyond the hospital entrance and admitting desk on what can be the noisiest hallway in the building. That's because a waiting area for pet owners is almost directly across the hall from me. Dogs and cats squirm in their owners' laps, in carriers, or at the ends of leashes. Turtles, guinea pigs, and rabbits crawl in the limited space of cardboard boxes, and birds peer out of their cages, singing and scolding. Couples, entire families, or complete strangers chatter together to pass time as they wait to hear about their pets' treatments, tests, surgery, and examinations. Veterinarians walk in and out, conferring with owners about an animal's prognosis or calling another owner into the hospital to begin a routine exam. I think most of our practitioners would find my office location far too distracting, but because my work is with people, for me it's ideal. If someone needs consolation while waiting for an animal's emergency treatment, has questions about the veterinarian's conclusions, or learns that his pet has died, I can talk to him on the spot or move across the hall to my office for more privacy.

One afternoon Lydia Hanson, a fifty-seven-year-old woman, stood in that hallway holding the body of her twelve-year-old beagle, Woody. He'd died in her arms on the way to the hospital for one of Woody's regular examinations when he suddenly gasped and went limp. Lydia arrived in a state of shock, insisting that he must only be unconscious. But our emergency service couldn't revive Woody, and Lydia couldn't seem to grasp the awful facts. She was crying, still shaken from her run to the hospital, and wavering between guilt and denial. First she'd sob because she thought she'd somehow strangled Woody as she carried him to the hospital; then she'd ask whether he'd wake up soon.

Her reactions were a natural result of the shock. Woody had been treated regularly for hypertension; he also suffered from cataracts and other old-age ailments. Lydia hadn't expected his death to replace this routine visit for medical care. Through her tears she mentioned how she dreaded going home to break the news to her husband, George. So I talked to her for more than an hour, until she felt able to return home. In that time Lydia explained just how valuable Woody had been to the Hansons.

It turned out her husband had recently gone through treatments and surgery for throat cancer; during his long recovery in the hospital Woody had been Lydia's only companion. The dog was waiting for her every day after she visited George and stayed by her side when she was home. "Without Woody I'd never have been able to endure the loneliness and worry," she told me. "He's always been loving, but when George was ill he made an extra effort to cheer me up." What's more, both Hansons had been diagnosed as being hypertensive, just as Woody had. I suspected this shared medical problem brought the couple closer to their dog and perhaps made his death more significant. Lydia could be expected to wonder whether her death, or George's, might happen just as suddenly.

Although she worried about how they'd get along without the dog's companionship, Lydia told me she and George had many people on whom they could rely for comfort and company. Their family included seven children, twenty-six grandchildren, and four great-grandchildren, many of whom lived nearby. Because the Hansons had lived in the same Philadelphia neighborhood for many years, they'd built strong relationships with friends and neighbors as well. Their friendship with Woody was important, but not because they lived in a social vacuum.

Still, Lydia's foremost concern as she sat in our waiting area was the adjustment to her loss. When she felt strong enough to go home I promised to call her and her husband the next day to see how they felt; I also urged her to call me whenever she felt her grief was too overwhelming to handle alone.

Lydia's worries *did* come true. George was extremely upset when she told him about Woody's death, and both of them cried for many hours, sometimes unable to believe their dog was gone forever. It took them three days to make decisions about handling his body, which Lydia had left at the VHUP. I discussed several options with them the day after Woody's death and they agonized for hours before choosing an autopsy and subsequent cremation for their dog. Because they made that choice without pressure, I think they were able to accept his death realistically. But their loneliness remained strong and their daily routines fell into temporary disarray. George's bedtime was between nine and ten o'clock; Lydia always stayed up until midnight or 1 A.M. with Woody to keep her company. Now she found herself crying late at night, unable to read, watch television, or sleep. Every move she made in those hours reminded her of Woody. To sleep at all, she told me, she had to take nonprescription sleeping pills; after she reported this to her physician, he prescribed a mild tranquilizer she could take during the day. For a few days she also lost her appetite and found she either confused facts or just couldn't remember them—all normal results of her depression.

George's most difficult adjustment came in the mornings, before Lydia was awake. He'd grown accustomed to rising early, feeding Woody, and playing with him before their early-morning walks. For several days George would get up, sit at the kitchen table, and cry until Lydia came downstairs for breakfast. And because his days began with anguish, they lost their purpose and patterns as well. Lydia and George found they spent more time together talking about their mutual grief but feeling too helpless to rectify it.

Fortunately, Lydia called me late on the first night after Woody's death to tell me about her sorrow and distress without her dog by her side. That phone call did more than offer her my attention and concern. It filled the void left by Woody's absence with some productive activity, a temporary substitute for his presence in the hours when her loss felt most acute. In the morning, at her suggestion, I called George just after he arose to help him cope in the same way. "This is my empty hour," he told me. So I asked him to describe the routine he and Woody had put together over many years; I encouraged him to cry when he faltered and listened to his concerns and fears.

Often, by the time George or Lydia had finished talking about their feelings, the empty hour had passed; Lydia would feel calm enough to try to sleep, and George would feel ready to begin his day. During our respective conversations I asked them to consider how they might subtly alter those routines. Perhaps George could try taking his morning walk before breakfast. Lydia might fill those late-night vigils with a phone call to a friend or read with music in the background when the house seemed so silent without Woody's presence. I also urged them to call their nearby friends and relatives for support, especially whenever they felt lonely. Gradually, I assured them, they'd be able to reorganize their habits and readjust to a life-style without Woody.

Both Hansons, separately and together, thought about getting another dog to reestablish their shattered routines. But, as many bereaved owners do, they hesitated, ultimately deciding to wait until they'd both resolved their loss. George spoke for both of them when he told me, "Getting another dog right now would be the same as saying Woody wasn't all that special to us, and that's just not true. Right now we're lonely because we'd rather have him with us, not because we just want any old dog. When we're ready we'll get another one."

Three weeks went by before the Hansons could establish a new life-style. Every day it was a little easier to talk about Woody without distress; their tears, depression, and sleeping problems subsided as they found and shared support. And because they made no decisions they might later regret, they found the new activities more comfortable and easier to accept.

You may be able to reconcile your pet's death in your

mind within hours, or you may need several days, weeks, or months to resolve your troubled feelings and resume a normal life-style. The mourning process and its rituals are just one part of that resolution. Although the burial or cremation you arrange will help you to accept your pet's death, you can't always expect to return to your usual routines immediately afterward. That's because your pet filled certain hours in your day as well as a particular place in your circle of relationships; you've lost not only the intangibles of friendship but a physical presence as well. The resulting gaps in your routine may be large or small, confusing or manageable, but they *will* remain to challenge you after your pet's death. Because your memories and other reminders of his absence can't be buried with him, they may complicate your recovery as well.

The subtle changes in your life after a pet's death are even more confusing because they trigger many different reactions. A haunting memory may further your guilt, disrupted routines may anger you, or the emptiness in your home may increase your depression. If you're considering another pet at this time the decision-making process can add other anxieties. These adjustments usually happen all at once, making the first few days after the death the most difficult. Allow yourself enough time to make clear decisions and realistic assessments of your situation so you can better face this challenge.

You'll read about how many other people chose to handle this phase of the healing process, but remember that your own choices depend on many individual, personal factors that won't match any other experience. Do only those things that make you feel comfortable, no matter what anyone else says or does in similar circumstances. I hope you'll find both ideas and reassurance in others' stories rather than compare yourself unfavorably as you read. Your control over your bereavement depends on your confidence in your own judgment at this crucial time; if you express your preferences and take action to meet your needs you can ensure a complete and satisfying recovery from your loss.

"The Whole House Seems Empty Now"

In the distress of bereavement you may find that the slightest reminders of your animal seem to trip you up, causing long delays in your recovery as well as wreaking havoc with your daily routine. It may have been pleasant to recall his odd habits, funny mishaps, and devoted companionship while he was alive, but his death ends that enjoyment, making you tearful, angry, depressed, or overwhelmed with guilt as you think about even the happiest memories. That's exactly what I mean when I say you have to *work* through bereavement. It's a struggle that may go on for a few hours or a few months, depending on your relationship with the pet. You're constantly pulled in two directions emotionally: you think of joyful past moments and yet can't feel that joy anymore. That's a natural response to your pet's death. In order to continue your life in a normal and regular manner you must try to put away these problematic reminders or use them to your advantage. You can avoid every thought of your pet after his death, thus eliminating the work involved, but I don't think you'll really recover if you choose to do that. It's far more helpful to face these challenges than to deny, in effect, that you have any reason to be upset.

Certain types of reminders seem to distress bereaving owners most often. It may help you to consider whether these common stumbling blocks will pose problems for you:

Memories Linked to Time. Like the Hansons, you may have relied on your pet's presence at certain times of the day, on particular days, or in special situations that existed regularly. Whether you did so consciously or unconsciously, you'll probably notice his absence most poignantly as you continue to go through those times now. For instance, if your animal was seriously ill you may have planned frequent visits to the veterinarian, given him medication at regular intervals, or even fallen into the habit of waking in the middle of the night to care for him. Every pet requires some pattern of attention from his owner, who must feed, exercise, groom, and play with him. You may have set aside a Saturday or Sunday to play with your cat or dog if you were usually busy during the week, cleaned out your gerbil's or rabbit's cage on a certain day, or simply become accustomed to the greetings and good-bye rituals your pet provided as you arrived and left home. The time you spent with him may not have been filled with activity; it's possible your pet's silent presence at the foot of the bed or by your side on the couch gave you comfort.

You may have to encounter these now-empty times after your pet's death to recognize how important they were, or perhaps you can already guess which ones will be the hardest for you. No one else can pinpoint them for you. Some people mourn the loss of regular activities, such as morning or evening walks, feeding times, or trips to the veterinarian. Others find they miss animals most on special occasions—a birthday, holiday, or vacation. Even the simplest, most mundane ritual can take on importance when a pet is no longer able to participate. One family found their saddest memories came when they served ice cream for dessert; their dog had always waited by the table for her chance to lick the almost-empty carton when they were through. No one in the family realized how much they'd miss that small after-dinner ritual. A woman who worked at home remembered her dog's absence whenever deliveries were made; she'd grown accustomed to restraining her large dog so he wouldn't scare the people bringing mail and packages. And almost every pet owner I've counseled has mentioned the pangs of loneliness they feel when they enter a silent house, no longer greeted by a cat or dog. Even if the time or situation doesn't seem important enough to upset you, remember that it's your associated memory of your pet that makes simple routines now seem more troublesome.

Physical Reminders at Home.   If you considered and treated your pet as a member of your family he probably acquired belongings and occupied certain places in your home—things and, of course, areas that remain after his death. Some are obvious: his cage, bed, collar, food dish, toys, and grooming tools. Others may be harder to identify right away because you took so many of his habits and actions for granted. A cat or parakeet might have perched on a favorite window ledge; a dog might have chewed a special toy or chair or slept in a sunny corner. Perhaps your pet played with your belongings, pawing at curtains, tearing books and magazines, gnawing on shoes. An outdoor cat or dog may have sought out certain yard areas, a climbing tree, or a shaded porch. All those physical items and places can seem incomplete after your pet dies; perhaps, as many pet owners say, "the whole house seems empty now."

You may have created some of those physical associations with your pet over the course of your ownership. Many people display their animals' photographs around the house; collect mugs, prints, books, and other objects with pet images; or install special items for the animal's convenience, such as cat doors and scratching posts, doghouses, and aviaries for birds. Perhaps you designated an area of the kitchen or den as the pet's place, putting his cage, bed, or food there. If he liked to follow you from room to room you can easily connect most of your surroundings with his presence.

Even if you store or give away most of your pet's belongings after his death you should realize that some permanent reminders will remain, bringing back sad memories. You might look out a window from habit, expecting to see your dog playing in the yard; continue to avoid sitting in the chair where your cat napped each day, or cry when you find yourself listening for a dog's bark or a bird's song. It's impossible to measure the difficulties these things present by looking at their ostensible significance. Again, it's the cherished association, not the actual thing or place, that's most important and troubling to you right now.

General Reminders.   You're as likely to encounter reminders in the world at large as you are in your home, but because you've taken so many of them for granted they may surprise you more. Television alone presents viewers with thousands of pet and pet-owner images on programs and commercials. Printed materials from books to greeting cards, posters to calendars carry similar messages. Public areas may prompt other memories: a park might remind you of walks with your dog, a stray cat on the street might resemble the one you lost. What's more, you'll see hundreds of other owners and their pets, as well as the businesses and products dedicated to animal care—pet stores, groomers, veterinary clinics, and the like. Almost every grocery or supermarket has a shelf, if not an entire aisle, stocked with pet foods and products. The sight of any of these might upset you after your pet dies because they mock your loss and throw it into high relief. You see real situations and images of the ownership others enjoy, without the satisfaction of having your own pet alive. The thought that you no longer have to buy food for him, transport him to the veterinarian, or arrange for grooming sessions may trigger tears and sadness—or just make you jealous of those owners who don't have to face the loss you're experiencing.

Because those other owners need and enjoy the same books, programs, stores, and resources that now cause your sadness, you may find it difficult or impossible to avoid these general reminders. Ignore or pass them by whenever you can; later, you should be able to encounter them with no more than bittersweet memories.

Three Methods for Accommodating Your Loss

Once you can identify the times, places, and objects that may trouble you during bereavement you're better prepared to work through the adjustment and reconcile your loss. Ideally the actions you take at this point should relieve some of your immediate distress as well as ensure your ability to function normally in the near future. That doesn't mean these actions will be easy, particularly if your grief is strong. But they will enable you gradually to regain control of your life on a day-to-day basis as you learn to live without your pet.

Although speaking or thinking about your deceased animal may be distressing—perhaps impossible—right now, your recovery will begin with the expression of your thoughts and feelings about him and his death. Talking or writing about your painful emotions will help you exert some control at a time when you sorely need some power over your fluctuating feelings. What's more, expressing your thoughts may help you to find the answers that seem to elude you. It's as simple as describing how you felt about your pet before his death; how the death came about; how you felt when you first knew he was dead, and how you feel now that he's no longer alive. You can write those thoughts and feelings in a letter to yourself or to someone else, or explain them in a conversation with a friend, relative, or counselor. As you've seen in the letters I've received, bereaved owners often describe their feelings in confused, rather than orderly, fashions. Don't worry about the clarity of your words at first; just say or write what comes to mind.

Once you've poured out everything that's on your mind, think about what you've said or written; look over the letter or ask your companion to repeat what you said. Have you confused some facts or exaggerated some feelings? What words can you add to make your thoughts clearer? Can you match certain events to the feelings that followed? Are you saying some words or phrases over and over and avoiding others? These simple questions can help you begin to understand your reactions. Your complete devotion to your pet before his death might explain your overwhelming feelings now; the manner of his death may have caused particularly strong emotions. The most important feelings are those linked to your loss, since you can make your life-style adjustments based on those reactions. If you described your sleepless nights after the death, lack of morning energy, or depressing loneliness in the evening, you've identified a problem area that's manageable, perhaps with some assistance and advice.

I hope you'll agree with the many others who tell me

that just expressing their feelings gives them some relief from their pain. What's more, your writing or talking may uncover ideas for dealing with your loss that you couldn't detect before. Other pet owners—whether they've gone through bereavement or have yet to do so —can often be most helpful in this situation. The supportive attention of someone who knows firsthand the pleasures and trials of pet ownership may encourage you to think even more clearly about your feelings. If you have no one to help you discuss your reactions and don't feel that writing will help you, you may want to contact a counselor, physician, social worker, or other professional; these people are available to listen as well as to provide help.

That's the second method for coping with your loss: finding and relying on support systems. Sometimes all the help you need during this period can be found within your existing network of relatives and friends. Another pet owner may be able to offer the most consistent, understanding support at this time, as well as contribute insights as you review your life with a pet. The same helpful encouragement might be found in a person who knew your pet well enough to think of him as a distinct personality. Such a person might be able to tell you things about your pet that you didn't notice or don't recall, especially happy moments that he shared with your animal. In general, other pet owners and people who knew and liked your pet in particular will be most likely to understand and accept your bereavement reactions, so you might want to turn to them first of all. These are people who can empathize, not just sympathize, with your loss. Beyond those personal resources you can consult with your veterinarian, physician, or family services organization. Pet bereavement counseling is available at the VHUP on the Penn campus in

Philadelphia and at the Animal Medical Center in New York City; similar programs are being considered at the University of Minnesota, the University of Tennessee, the University of California at Davis, Colorado State University, Louisiana State University, and the University of Wisconsin at Madison. You may live near one of these or other veterinary schools and should make use of any counseling service they might offer. To find a qualified counselor outside the veterinary profession ask your physician for a recommendation or contact one listed under "social services" in your local telephone directory.

In most cases, however, your grief and recovery will not require extensive analysis or therapy. You should simply seek a good and sympathetic listener, professional or not, who can accept your feelings and suggest ways to make them manageable. Choosing a professional to listen to your thoughts and emotions does not mean you're emotionally ill or incompetent—you may simply have no other source of support.

No matter where you find assistance you can ask for more than just a listening ear. Friends or family members might be willing to help you fill the "empty hours" left by your pet's death. Perhaps they can walk with you during the hours you reserved for walks with your dog; they might call or visit, at your request, to substitute for your pet's company. Someone can help you sort and store your pet's belongings, make funeral arrangements, or accompany you on a search for a new pet. If your pet's death leaves you alone in your house you may feel uneasy at night or at other times; a counselor or friend can offer to be available in case of emergency. You may never actually use these resources, but it's usually comforting to know they're available. And when someone courteously asks whether you need help during your bereavement you can make them feel more at ease by suggesting specific types of assistance they can provide.

Finally, as your feelings and thoughts become clearer and you're assured of some support, you can begin actively to adjust to life without your pet. Identify the routines, times, and places you associate most strongly with your pet. If, for instance, you always went home immediately after work to feed and play with him, you might begin to use that time to cook a special meal, to exercise, or to do errands. Perhaps, for a few days, you'd prefer to fill that hour by thinking or writing about your pet; later, you can replace that activity with a new one. Remember that it's *natural* to revert to your old routines—walking into the pet-food aisle in the supermarket, rushing home for your dog's evening walk, or scheduling regular veterinary appointments. Try to change your routines as soon as possible and move on to other tasks or activities. If necessary avoid situations and reminders that make you uncomfortable. Turn off the television program, leave the store, or walk away from the other owner with his pet if you need to. Keep reminding yourself that you can change long-standing habits only slowly and with effort. Your goal is to compensate temporarily for the empty hours and disrupted rituals until your pain has subsided. Eventually you can face any situation without distress.

"Would It Help to Get Another Dog?"

Betty, a thirty-four-year-old San Francisco biologist, had always thought of Bach as "a perfect dog." The shepherd-collie mixed-breed had been unable to walk without mechanical aids for almost a year; after several delays, Betty finally authorized euthanasia "because he seemed so unhappy." The decision came after ten years in which Bach became her "best friend, even before I was married," as she put it. "Everywhere we went people recognized me because of my faithful companion," she recalled. "He attended the classes I taught, went to labs and appointments with me. I never had to use a leash with Bach because he always stayed right by my side, even in enormous crowds."

It seemed, though, that Betty's great love and respect for Bach were delaying her recovery. "I cry about him at least once a day—I loved him so much!" she said. "I've spent the month since his death making a large scrapbook of his life, and every night I hold it and look at it and cry some more. I'm not sleeping or eating well, and although I've been exercising to relieve the stress, it doesn't seem to help much. Every time I read an article about dogs in one of my magazines or see them on the street or on TV, I cry again.

"Do you think it would help me to get another dog?" she asked. "I don't see how any dog could replace Bach, but maybe a different breed—not a shepherd-collie—would help to cheer me up. But sometimes I feel like a sick Bach would be better than no Bach at all, or better than any other dog. I don't know what to do; all I have now is nothing."

I wasn't sure Betty was prepared for another dog in her life; she hadn't fully accepted Bach's death. Her grief seemed too overwhelming to allow her to function normally, and a new pet might not benefit from that confused environment. But when I called her to discuss those issues she evaded them, resisting help. After I referred her to a qualified counselor in her area—at her request—several months passed before I heard from Betty again.

Her letter let me know she had bought a puppy after our last talk. "Kizzy's approaching ten months now, and has finally calmed down enough to give me a chance to rest!" Betty wrote. "Although she is entirely different from Bach, she's a good and loyal friend. And she has potential in lots of ways that Bach didn't. For example, she fetches all our newspapers from the bottom of the driveway, which I really appreciate on rainy mornings.

"I still think about Bach sometimes," she continued, "and I even had a dream about him the other night, but it was a happy one. Kizzy sure snapped me out of my feelings in a hurry because she needed so much attention. I lost two friends through death this year, and was especially grateful for her company at those times. It's been a terrible year of grief for me, but I'm just glad I've been able to get through it."

Kizzy's presence seemed to have been just the jolt Betty needed to accept Bach's death and to create a new life without her first "perfect dog." But no one can guarantee that kind of success. Betty took several risks in acquiring Kizzy so soon after her devastating loss; for some people getting another pet at this time may only increase the sadness and prolong the grief.

To determine whether a new pet will help you during bereavement, think about the situation in your household right now. Your feelings center on the animal who died and you're reminded of that loss in many ways every day. You may not have completely accepted the death yet. Now consider the animal you might bring into that situation. An untrained puppy or kitten, in particular, or any older pet that's set in his ways, requires training and patience. He needs time to adapt to your routines, and you need time to discover his. He can't duplicate the comfort, trust, love, and other benefits you developed over time with the pet you lost; eventually you hope to create new and different bonds with him, but those differences can be surprisingly annoying during your healing process. What's more, an animal's needs can't wait while you mourn your first pet. He'll need regular feedings, exercise, and attention even when you're angry, sad, or crying uncontrollably. If you ignore him or inadvertently direct some of your negative feelings his way he might misbehave and upset you further. So it's possible that what seems the easy solution —getting another pet—may also create the most problems for you.

The safest way to handle this dilemma is to wait before you acquire another pet, as the Hansons did. You can use this waiting time to consider the matter with care, from your point of view as well as that of the new pet. Are you older now, less willing or able to devote many hours to another pet's training and care? Has bereavement complicated your life enough for the time being? Would an animal soothe your troubled feelings or disrupt your life further? You may treasure your previous pet's companionship so much that no other animal could seem special to you; on the other hand, you may be one of many people who need and want an animal around at all times. Regardless of your preferences, waiting to make a final choice can't hurt you if you have some doubt about this matter. You face many confusing decisions if you want to choose a new pet carefully at any time—breed distinctions, temperaments, costs, care requirements, and many other considerations. Time may be necessary just to assess the most basic factors.

If you strongly desire to look for a new pet immediately, however, you still have options to consider. A mixed-breed dog might fit into your life as well as your purebred did; an older cat's less active habits may better suit your life-style at this time. Perhaps you want to acquire a different breed—or an entirely different kind of animal. Many people do feel comfortable in choosing another pet with the same breeding, age, and temperament as the one they lost through death. I suspect, however, that their choices are based on simple preferences rather than the desire to recreate an identical relationship. If your desire to find another pet is strong, and you know what you prefer, you can begin looking for one in confidence.

It's vital, however, that you pay attention to your feelings for the pet that died as you set out to choose another animal. Like George and Lydia, you may feel another pet would signify a lack of love and respect on your part for the previous animal. Getting another pet immediately after one dies doesn't really deny your first pet's importance. The new animal can't possibly replace the one you lost; if he could the death and this subsequent decision wouldn't seem so serious. Nor do your concerns about this option mean another pet is inappropriate or wrong—rather they demonstrate that you want to make a wise and caring decision.

Don't forget the final choice is yours. If you're offered a pet you don't want or aren't ready to accept you have every right to turn it down. When the decision involves more than one person it's wise to wait until all of you are in agreement; otherwise, your preferences are the only ones that matter.

So many people ask me to determine the "best time" to acquire another pet and I can't tell them what's appropriate because it's such a personal choice. That's why your family, friends, business associates, or neighbors shouldn't try to dictate the terms of this choice to you. Only you know all the factors. You should remind yourself you made numerous decisions about your pet before he died, trusting your good judgment and in-

stincts each time. Try to have that faith in yourself now.
If you consider your concerns first you'll find it difficult
to make a mistake with this decision.

"When Can I Expect to Recover from My Sorrow?"

Bereavement has a built-in frustration factor for most
people: as you experience guilt, anger, denial, or depression after a pet's death, and struggle to resolve those
feelings, you may wonder whether your pain will ever
end. Many owners ask me when they can expect that
sorrow to end, as if a schedule existed for these natural
and varying emotions. But no one can determine how
long your feelings will last; no matter how endless it
seems, you must continue to deal with your loss so that
you can resolve your hurt fully and effectively. If you
can acknowledge each emotion, accurately assess your
situation, and take action to remedy your pain, you need
not worry whether your grief will end—you'll be ensuring its end.

You can reassure yourself that you'll avoid further
problems and pain if you take the time to express and
cope with your feelings now. But if you're having trouble seeing your progress to recovery, think about what's
happened to you since your pet's death. How did you
feel last night? This morning? Now? Did you manage to
mention your pet's name or to talk about him without
crying today? Can you think about him calmly, if sadly?
Were you able to go to work and function normally?
Those seemingly tiny steps toward your recovery are
valid, strong signs that you're handling your bereavement well. Think, too, about the practical matters
you've faced since your pet's death—both in the healing process and your regular routine. Perhaps you're

now eating meals instead of refusing food or can calmly clean the house without getting upset when you see your pet's favorite places. You may have finally decided on a burial or made the cremation arrangements, watched television or had dinner with a friend rather than shun all activity. If you feel held back in your recovery efforts remind yourself of these particular accomplishments as the days go by to prove that you are indeed moving forward.

Many people realize they've recovered from an overwhelming grief when they can face a once-troubling situation—reminiscing about the pet that died, seeing a stray animal in the yard, or simply going about their regular business without depression. Recurring problems can in the same way indicate a stalled bereavement, one that may require additional help from formal or informal supporters if you can't correct the trouble by yourself.

Don't berate yourself for recovering too quickly or too slowly. Each individual needs a certain amount of time to handle this challenging mix of emotions, and you'll only feel worse if you think your progress doesn't match some improbable norm. Your relationship with your animal, built over years of living together, was distinct and personal—too special to be locked into a category now. You might also take comfort from the many others who've consulted me in their grief. An amazing majority doubt and agonize over their feelings and reactions, but once they face and resolve those emotions they find the experience helped them in some way. They may never have realized precisely why they cared about the pet and now cherish animals even more. Others find that the healing process makes them stronger, more capable of handling other tough situations; some say this first experience with grief put them in touch with feelings they could later draw on when a human friend or relative died. Perhaps the most surprised—and satisfied—of all are the owners who never expected to grieve so strongly but can now sympathize with others who feel awful when a pet dies. Their experiences—and their willingness to discuss them—make it increasingly acceptable for you to mourn the loss of a dog, cat, bird, horse, rabbit, or any other beloved pet animal. If you can confront your bereavement and resolve it you'll contribute to that growing understanding, perhaps making this experience easier for someone like yourself.

epilogue

The Significant Life
—and Death—
of Lady

by Bill Shaw

My dog lady, an Irish setter, was my pal, the one constant in my life when life wasn't predictable. During one four-year period I moved from Indianapolis to Tucson, back to Indianapolis, out to Santa Barbara, back to Tucson, north to Seattle, and back to Indianapolis again. My life was a mess. But through it all, I had Lady. She spent most of her time lying in the back seat of the car, sleeping the hours of travel away, content that I knew what we were doing. I didn't, of course, but that's the great thing about faithful dogs: They always believe in you. My friends thought I was nuts. Lady didn't. She always loved me, no matter what.

On a cold, drizzly night in November, 1980, our travels had taken us to a small, out-of-the-way town in Ohio. Napoleon, Ohio. It was a dreadful place under the best of circumstances, but we stopped anyway. After we checked into the Holiday Inn, we went for a quick walk. Lady darted onto the highway, running head-on to collide with a moving pickup truck.

The moment still burns in my memory, every frightful detail sharp and painful. The rain; the lights of the speeding truck; Lady, running blindly toward it; and the awful sound. Thump. Crack. Her neck snapped like a brittle twig, and she died instantly. I stood there in the rain, staring at her while the cars whizzed around her. My mind refused to accept what my eyes were seeing. Her eyes were open. She still looked alive. Surely she would get up now and walk back to the hotel with me. But she was dead, just like that: alive and frolicking one moment, dead the next. Gone forever from my life.

I instantly hated everything connected with my dog's death. The truck. The nice people who drove it. Napoleon, Ohio. The whole world. I had to hate something, anything, anyone because death is unfair—it must be *someone's* fault. It isn't, of course, which is why it's so hard to accept. Death just happens.

I tried to pretend it hadn't happened. I forced it out of my mind on the long drive home to bury Lady. To think about it would be to admit it. I knew that if I pretended hard enough, she would wake up. She was lying in the back seat as usual. For five straight hours I stared ahead, never looking back there. I played the radio, loud.

That night, alone at home, I cried. I don't think I'd ever cried before in my life. I cancelled appointments but never said why. People would think I was crazy to cry over a dog. After all, I was a grown man, and she was only an animal. There are lots of animals in the world, they'd say. Get another one. If it were that easy, why was I crying, not sleeping, not eating, not talking to anyone? What the hell was wrong with me? I thought I might really be going crazy this time, around the bend for good.

The more I thought about her death, the more I

blamed myself. I should have leashed her. It was my fault she'd died. Then I got mad at Lady. How could she be so stupid, running into a truck? Didn't she know how that would hurt me? Ungrateful dog. Then I felt guilty for feeling guilty, for crying, for everything. I was a mess, and this time Lady wasn't around to help me through.

Some well-meaning friends did gently suggest that I get another dog. I secretly hated them for their insensitivity. Lady wasn't just a dog. She was a friend, an irreplaceable soulmate. No dog could ever take her place, not ever.

I thought the pain would never end. But slowly, through the months that followed, it eased. Just a little bit each day. I've since learned from experts that a pet's death triggers a complex and bewildering set of emotions in the owner. Depression, tears, anxiety, and guilt are normal reactions. Everyone feels them. I wasn't alone. I wasn't crazy. Just normal. I didn't need to punish myself further by questioning my sanity for feeling those emotions. But I did. I hope I won't next time.

As time went by, the hurt was replaced by a true appreciation for the importance of pets in my life. For the first time, I realized just how significant Lady had been. She was a positive force, a good balance to everything else, especially when everything else wasn't going well.

Two years after she died, I got another dog, Dusty. Although no animal could ever replace Lady, her death made me a more sensitive pet owner. I think I'm a little nicer to Dusty—at least I try to be. I don't want to waste the time we have together. And when he dies, I'll know that it's okay to grieve. Maybe then it won't hurt so much.

The Last
Will and Testament
of an Extremely
Distinguished Dog

by Eugene O'Neill

I Silverdene Emblem O'Neill (familiarly known to my family, friends, and acquaintances as Blemie), because the burden of my years and infirmities is heavy upon me, and I realize the end of my life is near, do hereby bury my last will and testament in the mind of my Master. He will not know it is there until I am dead. Then, remembering me in his loneliness, he will suddenly know of this testament, and I ask him then to inscribe it as a memorial to me.

I have little in the way of material things to leave. Dogs are wiser than men. They do not set great store upon things. They do not waste their days hoarding property. They do not ruin their sleep worrying about how to keep the objects they have, and to obtain the objects they have not. There is nothing of value I have to bequeath except my love and faith. These I leave to all those who loved me, to my Master and Mistress, who I know will mourn me most, to Freeman who has been so good to me, to Cyn and Roy and Willie and

Naomi and—But if I should list all those who have loved me it would force my Master to write a book. Perhaps it is in vain of me to boast when I am so near death, which returns all beasts and vanities to dust, but I have always been an extremely lovable dog.

I ask my Master and Mistress to remember me always, but not to grieve for me too long. In my life I have tried to be a comfort to them in time of sorrow, and a reason for added joy in their happiness. It is painful for me to think that even in death I should cause them pain. Let them remember that while no dog has ever had a happier life (and this I owe to their love and care for me), now that I have grown blind and deaf and lame, and even my sense of smell fails me so that a rabbit could be right under my nose and I might not know, my pride has sunk to a sick, bewildered humiliation. I feel life is taunting me with having over-lingered my welcome. It is time I said goodbye, before I become too sick a burden on myself and on those who love me. It will be sorrow to leave them, but not a sorrow to die. Dogs do not fear death as men do. We accept it as a part of life, not as something alien and terrible which destroys life. What may come after death, who knows? I would like to believe with those of my fellow Dalmatians who are devout Mohammedans, that there is a Paradise where one is always young and full-bladdered; where all the day one dillies and dallies with an enormous multitude of houris, beautifully spotted; where jack rabbits that run fast but not too fast (like the houris) are as the sands of the desert; where each blissful hour is mealtime; where in long evenings there are a million fireplaces with logs forever burning, and one curls oneself up and blinks into the flames and nods and dreams, remembering the old brave days on earth, and the love of one's Master and Mistress.

I am afraid this is too much for even such a dog as I am to expect. But peace, at least, is certain. Peace and long rest for weary old heart and head and limbs, and eternal sleep in the earth I have loved so well. Perhaps, after all, this is best.

One last request I earnestly make. I have heard my Mistress say, "When Blemie dies we must never have another dog. I love him so much I could never love another one." Now I would ask her, for love of me, to have another. It would be a poor tribute to my memory never to have a dog again. What I would like to feel is that, having once had me in the family, now she cannot live without a dog! I have never had a jealous spirit. I have always held that most dogs are good (and one cat, the black one I have permitted to share the living room rug during the evenings, whose affection I have tolerated in a kindly spirit, and in rare sentimental moods, even reciprocated a trifle.) Some dogs, of course, are better than others. Dalmatians, naturally, as everyone knows, are best. So I suggest a Dalmatian as my successor. He can hardly be as well bred or as well mannered or as distinguished and handsome as I was in my prime. My Master and Mistress must not ask the impossible. But he will do his best, I am sure, and even his inevitable defects will help by comparison to keep my memory green. To him I bequeath my collar and leash and my overcoat and raincoat, made to order in 1929 at Hermes in Paris. He never can wear them with the distinction I did, walking around the Place Vendome, or later along Park Avenue, all eyes fixed on me in admiration; but again I am sure he will do his utmost not to appear a mere gauche provincial dog. Here on the ranch, he may prove himself quite worthy of comparison, in some respects. He will, I presume, come closer to jack rabbits than I have been able to in recent years.

And, for all his faults, I hereby wish him the happiness I know will be his in my old home.

One last word of farewell, Dear Master and Mistress. Whenever you visit my grave, say to yourselves with regret but also with happiness in your hearts at the remembrance of my long happy life with you: "Here lies one who loved us and whom we loved." No matter how deep my sleep I shall hear you, and not all the power of death can keep my spirit from wagging a grateful tail.